WITHDRAWN

P9-BXW-129

WITHDRAWN

THE GREEK TRAGEDY
IN NEW TRANSLATIONS

GENERAL EDITOR William Arrowsmith
CO-EDITOR Herbert Golder

SOPHOCLES: Antigone

SOPHOCLES

Antigone

Translated by
RICHARD EMIL BRAUN

OXFORD UNIVERSITY PRESS
New York   Oxford

OXFORD UNIVERSITY PRESS

Oxford   New York   Toronto
Delhi   Bombay   Calcutta   Madras   Karachi
Petaling Jaya   Singapore   Hong Kong   Tokyo
Nairobi   Dar es Salaam   Cape Town
Melbourne   Auckland

and associated companies in
Berlin   Ibadan

COPYRIGHT © 1973 BY RICHARD EMIL BRAUN

First published in 1973 by Oxford University Press, Inc.,
198 Madison Avenue, New York, New York 10016-4314
First issued as an Oxford University Press paperback, 1989

Oxford is a registered trademark of Oxford University Press

All rights reserved. No part of this publication may be reproduced,
stored in a retrieval system, or transmitted, in any form or by any means,
electronic, mechanical, photocopying, recording, or otherwise,
without the prior permission of Oxford University Press, Inc.

Library of Congress Cataloging-in-Publication Data
Sophocles.
[Antigone. English]
Antigone / Sophocles ; translated by Richard Emil Braun.
p.   cm.—(The Greek tragedy in new translations)
ISBN 0-19-506167-5 (pbk.)
1. Antigone (Legendary character)—Drama.
I. Braun, Richard Emil, 1934– .   II. Title.   III. Series.
PA4414.A7B7   1989   882'.01—dc20   89-22867

printing, last digit: 20 19 18 17 16 15 14

Printed in the United States of America

A vosotros que me ayudasteis
y a mis compañeros del palacio negro

EDITOR'S FOREWORD

The Greek Tragedy in New Translations is based on the conviction that poets like Aeschylus, Sophocles, and Euripides can only be properly rendered by translators who are themselves poets. Scholars may, it is true, produce useful and perceptive versions. But our most urgent present need is for a re-creation of these plays—as though they had been written, freshly and greatly, by masters fully at home in the English of our own times. Unless the translator is a poet, his original is likely to reach us in crippled form: deprived of the power and pertinence it must have if it is to speak to us of what is permanent in the Greek. But poetry is not enough; the translator must obviously know what he is doing, or he is bound to do it badly. Clearly, few contemporary poets possess enough Greek to undertake the complex and formidable task of transplanting a Greek play without also "colonializing" it or stripping it of its deep cultural difference, its remoteness from us. And that means depriving the play of that crucial *otherness* of Greek experience—a quality no less valuable to us than its closeness. Collaboration between scholar and poet is therefore the essential operating principle of the series. In fortunate cases scholar and poet co-exist; elsewhere we have teamed able poets and scholars in an effort to supply, through affinity and intimate collaboration, the necessary combination of skills.

An effort has been made to provide the general reader or student with first-rate critical introductions, clear expositions of translators' principles, commentary on difficult passages, ample stage directions, and glossaries of mythical and geographical terms encountered in the plays. Our purpose throughout has been to make the reading of the plays as vivid as possible. But our poets have constantly tried to remember that they were translating *plays*—plays meant to be produced, in language that actors could speak, naturally and with dignity. The poetry aims at being *dramatic* poetry and realizing itself in words and actions that are both speakable and playable.

Finally, the reader should perhaps be aware that no pains have been spared in order that the "minor" plays should be translated as carefully and brilliantly as the acknowledged masterpieces. For the Greek Tragedy in New Translations aims to be, in the fullest sense, *new*. If we need vigorous new poetic versions, we also need to see the plays with fresh eyes, to reassess the plays *for ourselves*, in terms of our own needs. This means translations that liberate us from the canons of an earlier age because the translators have recognized, and discovered, in often neglected works, the perceptions and wisdom that make these works ours and necessary to us.

A NOTE ON THE SERIES FORMAT

If only for the illusion of coherence, a series of thirty-three Greek plays requires a consistent format. Different translators, each with his individual voice, cannot possibly develop the sense of a single coherent style for each of the three tragedians; nor even the illusion that, despite their differences, the tragedians share a common set of conventions and a generic, or period, style. But they can at least share a common approach to orthography and a common vocabulary of conventions.

1. *Spelling of Greek Names*

Adherence to the old convention whereby Greek names were first Latinized before being housed in English is gradually disappearing. We are now clearly moving away from Latinization and toward precise transliteration. The break with tradition may be regrettable, but there is much to be said for hearing and seeing Greek names as though they were both Greek and new, instead of Roman or neo-classical importations. We cannot of course see them as wholly new. For better or worse certain names and myths are too deeply rooted in our literature and thought to be dislodged. To speak of "Helene" and "Hekabe" would be no less pedantic and absurd than to write "Aischylos" or "Platon" or "Thoukydides." There are of course borderline cases.

"Jocasta" (as opposed to "Iokaste") is not a major mythical figure in her own right; her familiarity in her Latin form is a function of the fame of Sophocles' play as the tragedy *par excellence*. And as tourists we go to Delphi, not Delphoi. The precisely transliterated form may be pedantically "right," but the pedantry goes against the grain of cultural habit and actual usage.

As a general rule, we have therefore adopted a "mixed" orthography according to the principles suggested above. When a name has been firmly housed in English (admittedly the question of domestication is often moot), the traditional spelling has been kept. Otherwise names have been transliterated. Throughout the series the -os termination of masculine names has been adopted, and Greek diphthongs (as in Iphigeneia) have normally been retained. We cannot expect complete agreement from readers (or from translators, for that matter) about borderline cases. But we want at least to make the operative principle clear: to walk a narrow line between orthographical extremes in the hope of keeping what should not, if possible, be lost; and refreshing, in however tenuous a way, the specific sound and name-boundedness of Greek experience.

2. Stage directions

The ancient manuscripts of the Greek plays do not supply stage directions (though the ancient commentators often provide information relevant to staging, delivery, "blocking," etc.). Hence stage directions must be inferred from words and situations and our knowledge of Greek theatrical conventions. At best this is a ticklish and uncertain procedure. But it is surely preferable that good stage directions should be provided by the translator than that the reader should be left to his own devices in visualizing action, gesture, and spectacle. Obviously the directions supplied should be both spare and defensible. Ancient tragedy was austere and "distanced" by means of masks, which means that the reader must not expect the detailed intimacy ("He shrugs and turns wearily away," "She speaks with deliberate slowness, as though to emphasize the point," etc.) which characterizes stage directions in modern naturalistic drama. Because Greek drama is highly rhetorical and stylized, the translator knows that his words must do the real work of inflection and nuance. Therefore every effort has been made to supply the visual and tonal sense required by a given scene and the reader's (or actor's) putative unfamiliarity with the ancient conventions.

3. Numbering of lines.

For the convenience of the reader who may wish to check the English against the Greek text or vice versa, the lines have been numbered according to both the Greek text and the translation. The lines of the English translation have been numbered in multiples of ten, and these numbers have been set in the right-hand margin. The (inclusive) Greek numeration will be found bracketed at the top of the page. The reader will doubtless note that in many plays the English lines outnumber the Greek, but he should not therefore conclude that the translator has been unduly prolix. In most cases the reason is simply that the translator has adopted the free-flowing norms of modern Anglo-American prosody, with its brief, breath- and emphasis-determined lines, and its habit of indicating cadence and caesuras by line length and setting rather than by conventional punctuation. Other translators have preferred four-beat or five-beat lines, and in these cases Greek and English numerations will tend to converge.

4. Notes and Glossary

In addition to the Introduction, each play has been supplemented by Notes (identified by the line numbers of the translation) and a Glossary. The Notes are meant to supply information which the translators deem important to the interpretation of a passage; they also afford the translator an opportunity to justify what he has done. The Glossary is intended to spare the reader the trouble of going elsewhere to look up mythical or geographical terms. The entries are not meant to be comprehensive; when a fuller explanation is needed, it will be found in the Notes.

ABOUT THE TRANSLATION

Richard Emil Braun, one of America's most promising younger poets, is the author of three volumes of verse: *Children Passing* (1962), *Bad Land* (1971), and *Foreclosure* (1972). He is also a distinguished scholar who is now professor of Classics at the University of Alberta. Besides this version of Sophocles' *Antigone*, Braun has done translations from the Greek of Theocritos and Herondas and from the Latin of Catullus, Horace, Propertius, and Ausonius.

The professional skill of Braun's poetry and the authority of his scholarship will be immediately visible. If the diction of his *Antigone* is appropriately muscular and flexible, the dialogue is rendered by a syntax that is often colloquially staccato (as a play of angry and opposed wills requires) but also capable of great force and dignity. The great Sophoclean lyrics require poetry of a quite unusual order—sustained but unobtrusive thought, exceptional musical control—and it is hard to imagine Braun's lyrics being bettered. Behind this professional handling of Sophocles' language and texture lies a cool critical intelligence and a fresh and coherent interpretation of the play. Finally, observant readers will note Braun's scrupulous responsiveness to Sophocles' structural symmetries and dramatic delineation of character—the family resemblance between Antigone and Kreon, the amiably circuitous narration of the terrified Sentry, and the final pathos of Kreon.

It is an impressive achievement. Here we have an *Antigone* which possesses real poetic and dramatic power; which is not marred by sentimental interpretation; a great Greek play which has not been simplified and archaized or, worse, modernized into spurious relevance. The achievement matters. For if we primitivize Sophocles in order to make him relevant to ourselves, we cut ourselves off from what he has to teach us, from skills we do not have, or are now losing, or need to refresh. It is to Braun's credit that he has avoided the pitfalls of relevance and the newly fashionable primitivism of scholars (who are too often unaware that primitive thought is not simple but astonishingly complex). Here, I suggest, we have that rare good thing, a truly tragic *Antigone*—not a tragedy of principles, but of human beings caught in the grip of principles which threaten to maim their humanity and defeat even the high courage of asserting principles in the first place.

Braun's *Antigone*, like Sophocles', is both beautiful and right; but she is also hard and, at times, unloving. For Braun understands that this is a matter of dramatic process. Step by step, he shows how Antigone, by opposing Ismene and Kreon, becomes hardened, concentrated on fulfilling the superhuman demands of the love she asserts. So too we see how his Kreon evolves, becoming his own, and his city's, worst enemy in his effort to protect it from those he thinks will destroy it. But above all Braun succeeds in re-creating the fundamental symmetry and irony of Sophocles' design: the terrible reciprocity of human existence, in which those doomed to division by condition and character come to accomplish, on themselves and one another, a tragic and recurrent fate.

Lincoln, Vermont   William Arrowsmith

CONTENTS

ANTIGONE

INTRODUCTION

I AUTHOR AND BACKGROUND

It seems that in March, 441 B.C., the *Antigone* made Sophocles famous. The poet, fifty-five years old, had now produced thirty-two plays; because of this one, tradition relates, the people of Athens elected him, the next year, to high office. We hear he shared the command of the second fleet sent to Samos.

When the people of Samos failed to support the government just established for them by forty Athenian ships, Athens sent a fleet of sixty ships to restore democracy and remove the rebels. The Aegean then was an Athenian sea. Pericles, the great political leader and advocate of firm alliance, was first in command.

Pericles' political, and Sophocles' poetic, authority had grown during Athens' expansion. Sophocles had been a close friend of the conservative Kimon, Pericles' chief political rival, who died in 449. Before his successful presentation of *Antigone*, Sophocles had become Pericles' friend.

In 444, when the Athenian people chose Pericles as their leader, they demanded greatness: democracy combined with imperialism. Periclean democracy meant free speech, free association, and open access to power limited by law; for, assuming that intelligence is born in all, law created by all is the best ruler. Imperialism—to which the Samian War is to be referred—meant wealth, the power to enjoy. If, moreover, enjoyment is itself a kind of power, it too must be limited by law: the law which defines enjoyment is beauty. Freedom, justice, and beauty are the components of greatness which the Athenians had chosen for themselves when they granted first literary acclaim, and then imperial duty, to Sophocles.

Sophocles and his fellow-citizens chose to widen democracy and extend imperialism. The alternative for the east-Greek peoples was oligarchy and Spartan influence. This choice—which the Samians tried to make for themselves—involved less exploitation, but far more repression. The inhabitants of oligarchic states lacked freedom and, often, beauty; instead, the principle of justice was rationalized by their apologists, who broadly used terms such as "order" and "stability," in which they claimed to find the essence of good rule. In this world climate, it is not surprising that the Athenians wished the author of *Antigone* to hold military office. A man who was so skilled was also wise. Sophocles might be expected to judge rightly and govern well should the cargo of free society, legal limits, and the acquisitive and aesthetic instincts shift and clash in the waves of crisis.

The few details of Sophocles' life that tradition provides combine in brief glimpses. Sophocles, for instance, must have known Anaxagoras and Herodotos; but how he affected them, or they him, is obscure. The sub-theme of custom vs. nature (*nomos–physis*) in the *Antigone* indicates that Sophocles was acquainted with contemporary sophistic teaching, but does not show what stand, if any, he took in this debate. An anecdote tells how once, during the Samian affair of 440, Pericles scolded the poet for showing more interest in a certain boy than in his war duties. Then again, in old age, we hear, Sophocles praised his impotence, likening himself to a slave who had at last escaped from a maniacal master. Finally, there is the tale that in 420, when Asclepius was brought to Athens to purify the city, Sophocles kept the god in his own house until a temple was built. From this, it appears likely that Sophocles was an officer of the cult of Asclepius. It is difficult not to believe that the author of *Antigone* was truly a healer.

With the *Antigone*, Sophocles began work on material that interested him for the rest of his life. A dozen years later—perhaps in the plague year 429, the year of Pericles' death—he staged *Oedipus Rex*. His last play, *Oedipus at Kolonos*, may have busied him up to that day in 406/5 when, it is said, as he recited from the *Antigone* to some friends, Sophocles died.

II   INTERPRETATION OF THE PLAY

In considering the *Antigone*, the reader should be aware of three restrictions: first, that the play is our main source for its story; second, that the *Oedipus Rex* and *Kolonos*, written at wide intervals long after, cannot be used safely to criticize events or characters in the early work; and third, that Sophocles was not Aristotle's pupil. The first stricture forces us to concentrate attention on the text itself, without precluding comparison with the Theban legends;[1] the second frees us from comparison in anticipation. (If I were concerned primarily with the later plays, I should start with Antigone.) The danger of Aristotelian criticism lies not only in its anachronism but in a basic confusion as to the purpose of poetry. Even were we more secure in our assumptions concerning Aristotle's own meaning, we could not understand Sophocles better for this. We would be, at best, seeing the poet through the eyes of one of his spiritual great-great-grandchildren, a less rewarding discipline, probably, than to regard him from our own viewpoint. Worse, we could be confining our judgment of poetry to the requirements of an irrelevant moral philosophy. Sophocles as poet showed what he believed to be actual. In Antigone, he presented the fall of the just and the evil consequences of good acts. The Antigone doubtless disgusted Aristotle (Poetics, 1452b, 4-6).

Until new evidence appears, one must presume that Sophocles invented many events in the story of his Antigone: (1) the form of Kreon's decree; (2) the quarrels between Antigone and Ismene; (3) the double burial of Polyneices by Antigone and the final cremation–burial by Kreon; (4) the love of Antigone and Haimon; (5) the entombment of Antigone; (6) Teiresias' intervention and Kreon's change of mind, and (7) the suicides of Antigone, Haimon, and Eurydice.

Some of these inventions pose problems: What is the poetic or dramatic purpose of the double burial? Why is the love story introduced at all, and then made known only when the action is nearly half over? Why is Kreon made, contrary to instructions, to bury Polyneices first and then proceed, too late, to try to save Antigone? Is Eurydice introduced merely to add to Kreon's sorrow? These are some of the questions that need to be answered chiefly from internal evidence.

The difficulties of the Antigone are due in large part to thematic complexity; this in turn is due to variety of vision, or duplication of viewpoint, partly inherent in the subject, then intricately schematized in treatment.

The Theban myths are stories of royal families. Such stories are, on the surface at least, necessarily split into public and domestic facts. This double aspect of the activities of its characters is obviously important in the Antigone. But here too it is well to remember that the Athenians believed the city-state was based on kinship. The poet's

1. See Appendix, pp. 95-98, where these legends are detailed.

vision is divided again when he interprets legend for his contemporaries. Sophocles deliberately anachronizes when Kreon is addressed as an Homeric king, and answers democratic arguments like an oligarch, while deporting himself like a tyrant.

Another complicating factor is the purely dramatic splitting of vision between audience and a variety of speakers. The characters do not merely act; far more, they comment on action, criticize motives, and judge ideas; all these moral utterances are astute or foolish, crude or gentle, intentionally or accidentally ironic, just as the author wishes. The vision of each character is limited in such a way as to enable the audience, with its wider perspective, to compare, criticize, and gradually assemble a composite vision. This audience is a viewpoint; like the characters, it is a part of the author's imagination. Sophocles' meaning exists in the ensemble of characters as it affects an audience of the Periclean age, which now, as then, exists in the imagination.

Despite its doublings of vision, the play is extraordinarily moving. Its humanity is never frozen into symbol. It may be taken as tribute to the success of the Antigone that it has been found next to impossible, by those who study the play, not to describe the characters as real people.

Assuming the originality of much of the story of Antigone, we can see that known portions of Theban myth may have been prototypes of the play's persons, events, and themes, and that these could have had clear relevance to the 440s B.C. as well as to general human nature.

Kadmos stoned "sown men" (Spartoi) and so incited them to fraternal war. Lykos imprisoned Antiope. I think it not unlikely that Kreon's decree (39-41)[2] and later entombment of Antigone (934-41) reflect those two bits of legend. One remembers too that Kreon, like Kadmos, loses his children, and seems also to abandon his throne. Laios exposed his son Oedipus, that is disowned and left him to die. Kreon disowns Haimon (914) when he calls him a slave, and effectively sends him to his death (918-21). Lykos, like Kreon, was regent before becoming king. Kreon's name—which can mean nothing but "the ruler," "the regent"—is provided by tradition; Sophocles takes advantage of this, for Kreon's rule is, if legitimate, ignoble.

The figures of Amphion and Zethos are also relevant to the Antigone. The brothers personify the arts of peace and of war, respec-

2. Line references throughout, unless otherwise indicated, are to my English version.

tively; and this dichotomy—certainly a vital one for Athenians of 441 B.C. when the price and rewards of empire were on the scales of conscience—is prominent throughout Sophocles' play. Again, the story of Amphion's Argive wife Niobe is used directly to illuminate the figure of Antigone, who applies the parallel to herself (979-85), then alludes (1017-18) to Argeia and Polyneices, in whom we may again see the misfortune of Amphion, destroyed by his marriage. The fact that Polyneices' name makes him a "fighter in many battles" and at the same time a "party in many quarrels" is noted by the Chorus (139-40) when they reproach him, in retrospect, for bringing war home from Argos.

The names Antigone and Haimon also seem part of the received legend. It appears that Sophocles took their meaning seriously, for he created an Antigone who, "born to oppose," relies on innate courage in facing tyranny, and he devised the manner of Haimon's death, where "blood" is poured wastefully forth.

It is not surprising that Teiresias appears in the Antigone. Any important occurrence in Thebes might demand the use of prophetic power; for any such event would probably attract the attention of those gods whom the Thebans considered their own. In fact, the gods who figure in the play are all participants in the story of Kadmos, where they appear in this order: Zeus, Apollo, Ares, Athena, Aphrodite, and Dionysos. What these gods do and mean in the Antigone will be considered shortly.

The Theban legends, from which Antigone was built, display a double vision of reality: action is divine and human. Human action, as noted, is subdivided into facts of public and of private life. In the human and public aspects there is special relevance to the 440s B.C. Here too the viewpoint is split. An Athenian might enjoy being reminded of ancient enmity between Boeotians and Peloponnesians. It is interesting, in this regard, that Sophocles does not presuppose or prepare the Attic tale of Theseus' intervention in Thebes and enforcement of burial of the Argive war dead. (Teiresias seems to allude to this possibility in 1170-7 and 1257-9. Kreon, however, does in fact bury Polyneices, and so removes the motive for Theseus' famous settlement.) Sophocles suppresses a flattering tale and eliminates Theseus as a potential hero ex machina. His intention in so doing is surely that he wanted his Thebes to represent more than the Thebes of history, and its people to struggle with problems which no clever intruder could solve simply. Here are no tricks of popular appeal.

The Thebes of Antigone is an image of the city-state. As such, it must show some public facts of importance to Periclean Athenians: these facts are ideas in conflict. Kreon (809-18) expounds a tyrannical and oligarchic, Haimon (837-62) a democratic view of law and leadership. The combining of tyrannical and oligarchic in Kreon is a peculiar pairing of different, though logically compatible, concepts of government; though few oligarchs would have admitted the compatibility, many democrats might insist upon it. Kreon's laws are his own; the principle behind them is obedience to power, their alleged purpose is stability, their apparent motive power-hunger. Haimon's principle is reason, his motive love for Antigone. Haimon, democracy, Eros; Kreon, autocracy, Ares—the diagram has appeal. Kreon is a military leader who is not governed by civil norms. An Athenian general, however, had to render an account of his acts to the people. Athenians associated law with freedom from autocratic rule; laws, to Pericles, were the enactments of the majority of citizens duly assembled.

In this play, Antigone obeys a law which the citizens, as a whole, approve. In order to do so, she must die under Kreon's edict. (It is important to recall that in Aeschylus' *Seven Against Thebes*—the only extant tragedy on this theme before the *Antigone*—it is a *democratically voted* interdict which denies burial to Polyneices, though without specifying a penalty for disobedience.) Antigone suffers what any individual risks who asserts freedom under tyranny, or individualism against pressure to conform. For this act of public heroism, her motive is domestic. Never does she give a political explanation of her deed; on the contrary, from the start she assumes it is her hereditary duty to bury Polyneices, and it is from inherited courage that she expects to gain the strength required for the task (42-4). Antigone's public virtue is the product of personal loyalty.

Kreon, by contrast, turns from political to domestic tyranny, then justifies the first with analogies to the second. Declaring (222-3) the worthlessness of anyone who "cherishes an individual beyond his homeland," he denies his nephew burial. Then, refusing to pardon his niece, his son's fiancée, Antigone, he claims (798-807) that he must kill her to preserve public order and to uphold law, which he equates with the rule of the strong. At present, Kreon is a political tyrant; probably he has long been a domestic one. By this time, a modern audience might decide that the dichotomy—public and private—is more apparent than real. The two aspects appear inseparable and interactive. Athenians would have had no doubt: their city-state was assumed to be fundamentally a kinship unit.

Not unrelated to the theme of autocracy and freedom is that other duality, divine and human. The Theban legends emphasize six major deities; the persons of the Antigone tend to interpret one another and explain phenomena with reference to these gods. Both Kreon (224) and Antigone (550-1) assume the approval of Zeus; to Kreon, he represents power, to Antigone justice. Yet, Antigone attributes her family's misfortunes to him (6-8), and Kreon blames his ruin on an unnamed god (1467; could he be Eros?). The Sentry and Chorus (314-26, 350-1) assign the first burial of Polyneices to the gods; Kreon denies this categorically. The onlooker is convinced the characters believe what they say when they say it, but cannot tell which among them is right. The gods are unreliable, their role ambiguous. Teiresias, presumably representing Zeus and Apollo, appears too late to avert disaster: if the gods do not clearly intervene there, one doubts that they intervened at the beginning. The Chorus twice (first and fifth stasima) pray to Dionysos in vain. Eurydice is prevented from seeking Athena's aid (1363-7).

There remain Ares and Aphrodite. These are, in Antigone, at least as much symbols, War and Love, as gods; but there is no doubt they are personally active in the play. When one thinks, first, that the daughter of these two was Harmonia (Kadmos' wife in the legend), and then hears the central ode (942-57) where Love "conquers" and drives men mad, the difference between Love and War seems justly minimized by the Chorus; one is tempted to see the two as a pair. Love, which inspired Haimon to speak on behalf of Antigone, and had prompted Antigone to heroic action, also caused their deaths. Love seems no less a destroyer than War.

But this must be nonsense; and, before the play ends, it appears so. Love is blamed by the Chorus while Kreon rules. That is, the very conditions of the play which make it a tragedy are abnormal. It is not normal to deny anyone burial, one's nephew still less, or to bury one's niece, or anyone, alive. Neither is it normal for Love to destroy, or for War only to rescue. In the parodos, the Chorus thank Ares for Ares will return as a destroyer. Kreon is to blame. He knows Ares well, saving Thebes; but Thebes has not been saved. "Harmony" is absent. but Aphrodite not at all, and so separates them. He exposes this ignorance when he says (703) that it makes no difference who marries whom. His thoughts, as his manner of speech shows, are full of Ares; his conception of government is militaristic, "Spartan," one is tempted to say. Kreon made Love seem, to the Chorus, the same as War. The gods, here, seem indifferently to be forces which affect men, and forms of human feeling and action.

Human and divine, like public and private, may be the dual images of an integral object. The *Antigone* displays schematic pairing and antithesis in structural detail as well as in idea. The Theban myths are well suited to double vision, to curious couplings, and to division of natural pairs. Minos and Rhadamanthys, Zethos and Amphion, the metamorphoses of Teiresias—each a two-in-one relation of a different sort—suggest even more complicated relationships within the legend at the point where *Antigone* begins.

Eteokles and Polyneices, and their sisters, Antigone and Ismene, are children of Oedipus and his mother Jocasta; the two pairs are the brothers and sisters of Oedipus, their father, and the grandchildren of their mother Jocasta. The two boys have been sundered in rivalry for power, and have killed each other in single combat. Kreon, by decree, has sent Eteokles to the Underworld and kept Polyneices in the upper air; the one, buried, is free, while the other, left exposed, is confined. Similarly, during the war, one of Kreon's two sons, Megareus (or Menoikios), has died by his own hand and temporarily saved the city; the other, Haimon, survives, but will, at the end of the play, also die by suicide, after failing to save Antigone. When the play begins, then, Antigone and Ismene have been parted from their brothers, and Haimon has been separated from Megareus, by death, while Eteokles and Polyneices, united in dying, have been divided in death.

In the first scene, Antigone and Ismene quarrel and part. The Chorus invoke Zeus, Ares, and Dionysos. Kreon enters, hears of the first burial of Polyneices, and accuses and dismisses the Sentry. The Chorus sing an ode about the dual nature of mankind: like the gods in daring, but mortal; and possessing equally great potential for evil and good.

Schematic pairing continues as the Sentry returns to report the second burial and the capture of Antigone. The second and final dismissal of the Sentry is followed by a second and final break between Antigone and Ismene, both of whom Kreon considers guilty. The Chorus sing about the fall of men and the eternal power of Zeus, concluding that when gods destroy a man they cause him to confuse good and bad, one for one. Next, Haimon and Kreon talk. This is the center of the play; at the exact center is Kreon's claim that obedience to leaders saves men's lives in battle. Kreon condemns Antigone and drives his son away. The Chorus sing of Love under two aspects: gentle and inescapable, a playful conqueror and an eternal law. Antigone also considers Love and War as she goes to her prison, comparing herself to Niobe and further noting that Polyneices died in war because of his marriage in Argos, while because of this she must herself die unmarried. The ensuing ode alludes to the power of Zeus and of Dionysos, and the indifference of Ares to human suffering.

The Teiresias scene also is in two parts. The first part mirrors both the Sentry's report of the first burial and Haimon's interview with Kreon. Like the Sentry, Teiresias is accused of taking bribes, when, using arguments similar to Haimon's in the plea for Antigone, he asks Kreon to bury Polyneices. In the second half of the scene, Teiresias tells Kreon his crime is double.

The Chorus call upon Dionysos for the second and last time. The Messenger, like the Sentry at his second entrance, finds the Chorus alone; then, just as the Sentry was joined by Kreon (468), the Messenger is met by Eurydice (1359). He tells first of the cremation–burial of Polyneices, then of the second and final parting of Kreon and Haimon, that is the death of the latter. He concludes that the dead are joined together. Haimon and Antigone are together, but Polyneices and Eteokles, Haimon and Megareus too, are all now on the same side of the earth. When Kreon returns, Eurydice has died. Kreon is led into the palace, where only Ismene remains.

The *Antigone* seems compounded of pairs which life sunders: Eteokles and Polyneices, Megareus and Haimon, Ismene and Antigone, Kreon and Haimon, Antigone and Haimon. The last, the most vital pair, never meet during the play. This somber keynote—doomed pairs—is sounded by Ismene (56-72): Oedipus and Jocasta begin the tale, and Kreon may end it with Ismene and Antigone. Parting is the doom life offers. This is the dramatic lesson of the prologue, where Antigone and Ismene disagree almost from the start; there is no hint of such a break in Aeschylus' *Seven*—it is evidently Sophocles' invention.

Death, on the contrary, unites and reunites. This is a fact of faith for Antigone (1047-51) as she faces death: she will join her father, mother, brothers; though she does not now know it, her tomb will be her wedding chamber (1436-7). Those who die are reconciled. Kreon and Ismene, who alone survive the action of this play, remain separate and solitary.

Why, if death cancels rifts, can life not do so? Surely because, in the world of the *Antigone*, love is absent from life. Kreon is responsible. It is he who parts what should be inseparable. The Chorus repeatedly see, in the play's grim partings, the operation of the curse of Laios, but attach the hereditary guilt to Antigone. This is doubtful. The same old courtiers blame Love—in the third *stasimon*—for quarrels. The true heir to Laios' fault is Kreon. The curse is nothing supernatural, but rather a repetition of human evil by a man too foolish to mark the warnings of family history.

Laios first betrayed Pelops, king of Argos, then exposed his own son, Oedipus; in so doing he created enmity with the Argives, and defiled his own home. Kreon, who had abetted Eteokles' treacherous usurpation of the Theban throne, and who allowed his son to die in the course of the consequent war, insulted dead Polyneices along with the Argive dead, then disowned his younger son and buried his niece alive. Kreon chose two ways to Laios' one, to exacerbate Argive hostility, and five ways to violate his own family's sanctity. Kreon is Laios' ape and his exaggeration. Betrayal of faith and disregard of family bonds are the themes of Kreon's reign. Permeated with hate, life lacks cohesiveness; the polar opposite of life, the anti-world of Hades, must then contain love.

The play begins with a burial, that of Eteokles, and a denial of burial to Polyneices (26-33). The end is similar: Kreon burns and buries Polyneices (1386-97) and opens Antigone's tomb (1398-9; though Haimon had broken in, the entrance was still blocked). Kreon leaves Antigone there, though he has hoped to lead her back living; Haimon, whom he hoped to call away (1422-4), he carries home dead. When Kreon buries Eteokles he begins tragic events; when he exhumes Antigone, he ends them.

In the first third of the play, there are two further burials, of Polyneices. The first, when made known, shows Kreon as a tyrant who attributes an act, which others feel is divine, to greed for money. Kreon's crudity, in this regard, is still clearer later (1193-1209) when he accuses Teiresias—who has asked him, on plain grounds of piety, to bury Polyneices—of the same venality. The second burial of Polyneices shows that Antigone, not conspirators, did the deed, and not for money, but for love. Kreon rejects love when he condemns his niece.

While Antigone was prompted by her love to fulfill a religious duty, Haimon is inspired to political activity, to argument. Kreon rejects with militaristic slogans (798-824) the democratic and humane views Haimon presents. Kreon's speech, again, is the center of the play: love's arguments are opposed by Kreon with notions of statecraft drawn directly (cf. 224-9) from command in wartime. At the close of the episode (934-41) Kreon orders Antigone's burial. Then in the ode which directly follows, when the Chorus hymn Love, one is reminded that Antigone has called Kreon's decree martial (39-41). The defeat of Love—as Eros, Aphrodite, in the family and the state—is central to the play, in meaning as in location.

If the first burial lets Kreon discount the divinity of a reverent act, the second burial lets him argue, again wrongly, against love, and to rout and drive Love from himself and from Thebes. In 625-41, Kreon can only transfer his political cliché, the double duty of rewarding friends and harming enemies, to the case of Eteokles and Polyneices. His public argument has no place for love, since his public acts are in fact dictated by the spirit of enmity. Antigone realized this from the start (12-15). When Teiresias reports bad omens and urges Kreon to relent, his account includes a description (1151-7) of the augural birds attacking each other: they are virtually at war, because of Kreon's policy. As Kreon's suppression of love has created civil disharmony and destroyed his home, it has also interposed strife between men and the normal access to divine knowledge.

Antigone's devotion to her brother is truly a kind of reverence (1020). She, who (642-3) was born to love both her brothers despite the rift between them, has had the sharpest insight into Kreon's error of fission (cf. 210-11). In 515-18, she is compared by the Sentry to a mother bird: such is the nature of her concern for Polyneices. When she leaves for the tomb, Antigone bewails her childless state (1072-5). Does she think, as death approaches, that she has been wrong? This is another double focus on love. The love that made Antigone bury Polyneices is a moral force; the love she regrets in the kommos is a natural force: both together are the "mandate" of the third stasimon. Antigone is certainly not at "fault." She obeyed love vis-à-vis Polyneices; she did not thereby reject the living love of Haimon. She had no choice in the first, and was prevented by Kreon from choosing the second; Antigone "feels pain" only for the second, though it was for the first that, to avoid pain, she dared and dies.

The question of Kreon's choice in disposing of Polyneices before seeing to Antigone is treated in the note on 1389-98. Kreon cannot understand that the law he has broken is not what tradition, the "established laws" (1292), ordains, but is the force of Love (or of Justice) which moves these laws and makes them sacred. He reverts, instead, to his initial precepts: that the homeland is most important, the individual least (222-3), and that it is the stability of the state that makes love possible (228-9). Kreon has turned the business backwards. He may obey the letter of traditional law, and bury Polyneices; but the spirit, which is love, family feeling, and loyalty, he ignores still. Kreon's last error, then, is his first. He learns this in Antigone's tomb. As he hurries there, he still divides love from the law by which he lives.

As to Eurydice, I have hinted in the résumé (p. 11) that she is a kind of double of Kreon. The "marriage in Hades' house" Kreon originally suggested (to Antigone, 644-6, then to Haimon, 794-5) has been consummated (1436-7). The death of Antigone and Haimon has, as its offspring, the death of Eurydice. As I have noted, Kreon's entry early in the play (468) corresponds to Eurydice's (1359). In the first, Kreon returns as the Sentry tells the Chorus that Antigone is guilty of burying Polyneices. The Sentry completes his report to Kreon, who thereupon resolves to execute Antigone. As a result of this resolve, Kreon condemns himself, as well as Antigone, to a living death. When Eurydice enters, at an approximately corresponding position toward the end of the play, the Messenger is telling the Chorus of Haimon's death. He completes the tale, adding Antigone's suicide, to Eurydice, who then consigns herself to death. She dies cursing Kreon, not for Haimon's only, but for Megareus' fate as well. The dual scheme is completed: Kreon cursed himself when he ordered Antigone to be punished.

The original sentence was stoning, but Kreon changed it to immuring in order to avert a curse from the city (934-7). Perhaps the change of sentence also represents a retreat in policy forced on Kreon. (Again note: no penalty is specified in the Seven Against Thebes.) Haimon had said the people of Thebes approved Antigone's deed (839-50). Public stoning, in which the whole community could participate, was punishment for public enemies. If the Thebans would refuse to take part in such an event, Kreon is well advised not to require it of them. But here too the two-in-one scheme is a picture·of Kreon's reversed understanding. Teiresias emphasizes the direct reversal of nature (1240-7), which is, however, typical of Kreon's thinking. Kreon's "principles" are themselves blameworthy (1171). Teiresias, moreover, is a technician, an augur; he finds Kreon's wrongdoing formally offensive. By the doubled crime of separation, of keeping Polyneices in the light and segregating Antigone (cf. 55) from the living, Kreon has interfered both with gods of the Underworld and with the Olympians in their respective domains. The mechanical nature of Kreon's offense is characteristic. It is also, in its duality, typical of the whole play. By offense to the gods of the netherworld, Kreon finally offends Zeus (1170-7; 1202-5).

Yet, in a sense, Kreon did not change the sentence. When an outraged community stoned a public enemy, it performed a kind of burial rite, covering and concealing the offender. When Kreon pronounces doom on Antigone (934-5) he has her "hidden . . . in a rock hollow"; when he seeks to exhume her, it is from stone (1398-9). Moreover, we know that the enemy of the people is not Antigone, but Kreon. When he buries Antigone in stone, Kreon is himself, in his estimation, the community, the state (cf. 885-9); but Kreon buries, with Antigone, his better self, and does so in the presence of the horrified citizens. He hopes, by a technicality, to cover guilt; really, he stifles conscience.

Teiresias says (1148) that Kreon is walking "the razor's edge." Kreon's balance, clearly, has failed him more than once. Kreon falls away from love; by his martial statecraft, he wrecks the stability he has sought for the community; he loses his home through tyranny. His domestic and public crimes are complementary and inseparable. To show this appears to be the main purpose of the double confrontation between Ismene and Antigone, Ismene and Kreon (651-718).

Kreon begins the scene, saying he has nursed twin plagues, a pair of traitors, in his home. One wonders what that home is like, and suspects Kreon's understanding of his sons, as well as of his nieces. One may also abstract his words from the immediate context, and think the two girls represent rebellion and submission, positive and negative. Antigone rebels for a reason Kreon fails to understand. Ismene cautiously submits, without approving Kreon's ideas or actions. One thinks that, like the Chorus, Ismene will abandon Kreon at the play's end. This is the tyrant's handicap: the brave rebel, while the prudent stand by to bear witness; the former may actually destroy him, while the rest allow him to corrupt and destroy himself (cf. 837-8, 858-60). Kreon's condemnation of both sisters seems an unconscious act of ironic justice; it shows the tyrant is as deadly to those who permit him to misrule as to those who try to stop him; and it suggests that Kreon may be half aware that the subject loyal to his rule is essentially a traitor to his potential for good.

When Ismene asks Antigone (673-4) what life will be worth without love, the answer points to Kreon. The implication is that Kreon and Ismene are destined to live on, after the play ends, bereft of all they love or should love. Antigone does not know this: Sophocles gives the words weight. Antigone does know, and seems here to mean, that Kreon, by depriving life of love, has emptied it of value. In this episode, Antigone and Ismene are split apart for the second time. The two scenes (47-125; 657-91) are mirror-images. In the prologue, Antigone invited Ismene to risk death with her; now Antigone rejects Ismene's offer to be her partner in death. Ismene refused then; now Antigone refuses. Antigone chose to risk death rather than live without love, for to abandon Polyneices' need would have been to abandon her love of him; accordingly, the death she risked was meaningful (120-2). But Ismene chose to live on without love (cf. 683), and would now choose a useless, seemingly meaningless death. She feared death, and so would not help Antigone; now that she cannot help, she fears life. The scheme completes itself.

When Ismene pleads for Antigone's life, to Kreon, she starts with the same question (698-9): how can she live without Antigone? Kreon says to forget her. Then Ismene asks about Haimon: if Kreon can despise the girl his son loves, he does not love his son. Kreon does not. But elsewhere Kreon seems to seek love. When Haimon enters, Kreon asks him, "Do you love me" (770-1) "whatever I do and how?" Kreon has confused love with obedience before this. After the first burial of Polyneices, Kreon contrasted the behavior of discontented citizens with what they should do: "properly shouldering the yoke . . . which is the one way of showing love to me" (369-70). He tested the Thebans' love with his decree, and found it wanting; now, as he sentences Antigone for defying the decree, he finds Haimon's love hollow. Kreon is to be pitied for his incomprehension. What he seeks is the love of beast for human master; he has, himself, no love to give, only commands.

Even cruel Ares loved, though—loved Aphrodite. One should, therefore, not be shocked when Kreon leaves the stage heartbroken. Until Haimon dies, and Eurydice, he seems capable of no emotion but anger. When he condemned Antigone, he said that with her death he had "everything" (606). Now, he prays for his own death, which is everything he still wants (1522). This is convincing; it is disturbing too: the man is a man, and he is to be pitied. One must blame him; but as he blames himself, one wonders. Did he, after all, love his wife and son? He did, and did not know it; he could not know that in which he did not believe.

If we sympathize, at last, with at least the humanity of Kreon, it is less easy to excuse the Chorus. The old courtiers learn wisdom late; perhaps, like Kreon, too late. They, however, are not fools; in their songs they have shown subtlety and learning. Yet these men excused and supported Kreon's folly until Kreon, in effect, gave up his authority (1268-77). Though they knew what law is, and though they worshiped Love as well as Ares and Dionysos, nevertheless, even while they grieved for her, they blamed Antigone for her doom. When they might have used their eloquence to plead with Kreon, they soothed their own conscience with the easy lore of hereditary curses. Kreon puts these men in their place justly when he tells them (713) that they, as well as he, have determined Antigone's death. It was their own free will that they denied, not Antigone's, when they remained so long locked in silence by fear. The play's most alarming double-focus fixes the men of the Chorus, who see truth but do not face it.

When the old gentlemen of the Chorus persisted in regarding Kreon's edict as law, they were not playing the part of conservatives, in the finer sense; they were merely being cautious. "A law," they say in effect (247-52), "is law until it is changed." Ismene, perhaps only because of her proximity to the case, did regard the decree as unjust, but considered it necessary to obey (97-8) as long as others did so. This, then, is the plea of the callous and of the weak: conformity.

Antigone opposed conventional piety to Kreon's edict. Her proposition (550-64) was that a law must not violate morality. Haimon, on the other hand, appealed to the consensus of men: his was a democratic argument, based on the belief that a law must be in harmony with the considered opinion of the citizens. The personal motive of both Antigone and Haimon in opposing Kreon happens to be identical: love. In this play, traditional morality and majority opinion happen to agree; that this is a love match not made daily is shown by the *Seven Against Thebes*.

We may conjecture that, to Sophocles, the question of democracy vs. autocracy was more basic than piety vs. secular law. In the *Antigone*, he seems to approve religious tradition as a moral guide because, like consensus, it offers likelihood of truth: tradition is tested temporally, consensus also numerically, the first through changes of custom, the second by diversity of individual ideas. The greater probability that Kreon, in his tyrannical isolation, would be wrong, is demonstrated when he shows himself to be wrong; the advantage of democratic consensus is, here, emphasized by its endorsement of pious tradition.

Sophocles does, however, admit that religion contains troublesome ambiguities: piety may demand right behavior, but the gods themselves are not reliable guides to what is right. Teiresias, one remembers, appears too late. Similarly, Sophocles does not ignore the possibility of mass human error; the majority of Thebans, like Ismene, agree with Antigone, but obey Kreon. Fearing Kreon, the people fail Antigone, who is thereby as isolated in her rectitude as Kreon is insulated in his perversity. Freedom needs strength as well as sensitivity. The popular attitude toward Kreon is that of the Sentry, whose terror neither stifles his disapproval (392-404) nor slows his obedience (408-13, 527-37). From this, one may guess that Sophocles recognized that the rights of the exceptional individual are precious, at least when, as with Antigone, such rights confirm the freedoms which the majority continue, even secretly, to approve.

To us, to whom Kreon's flagrant misdeed is his invasion of personal and conscientious rights, Sophocles says this much: neither should the ordinary individual, who is wrong, rule the majority, who are passive, nor should the extraordinary individual, if right, acquiesce. The tragic problem of popular rule—where free citizens seem to violate by consensus the rights of minorities and of individuals, unusual and ordinary —is only suggested. The Antigone's complacent courtiers abet one tyrant, and become, in effect, a board of tyrants. We know their like in institutions, agencies, departments, and bureaus, which, for the sake of "the law till it is altered," and such generally accepted purposes as health, defense, education, and finance, erode freedom. Until such old men learn wisdom, Antigones will be "born to oppose," who, unless gentleness prevails, will be driven again and again even by the Choruses of democracy, either to civil disobedience or to criminal withdrawal.

The text I have followed is R. C. Jebb's in Sophocles, Part III: The Antigone (Cambridge, 1891), supplemented by A. C. Pearson's in Sophoclis Fabulae (Oxford: The Clarendon Press, 1924). Jebb's prose version and commentary proved consistently valuable.

I wish to thank the General Editor for generous help. No one acquainted with his work is in danger of blaming him for the faults of mine.

Edmonton, Alberta   RICHARD EMIL BRAUN
1966, 1972

ANTIGONE

CHARACTERS

ANTIGONE daughter of Oedipus and Jocasta
ISMENE sister of Antigone
KREON king of Thebes, brother of Jocasta
HAIMON son of Kreon and Eurydice, fiancé of Antigone
TEIRESIAS the prophet
EURYDICE wife of Kreon
SENTRY
MESSENGER
KORYPHAIOS chorus leader
CHORUS of elderly Theban nobles

Attendants, armed slaves, boy

Line numbers in the right-hand margin of the text refer to the English translation only, and the Notes at p. 75 are keyed to these lines. The bracketed line numbers in the running headlines refer to the Greek text.

A square in front of the Theban palace. The palace faces south. In the fore-
ground is an altar. This is the hour of dawn. As the action proceeds, the area
gradually brightens. ANTIGONE *waits on the audience's side of the altar.*
ISMENE *comes forward from the palace and approaches hesitantly.*

ANTIGONE Ismene?
Let me see your face:
my own, only sister,
can you see
because we are the survivors
today Zeus is completing in us the ceremony
of pain and dishonor and disaster and shame
that began with Oedipus?
And today, again:
the proclamation, under the rule of war   10
but binding, they say, on every citizen. . . .
Haven't you heard? Don't you see
hatred marches on love
when friends, our own people, our family
are treated as enemies?

ISMENE No, Antigone,
since the day we lost our brothers,
both in one day, both to each other,
I haven't thought of love—happy or painful, either.
Last night the enemy army left.   20
I know nothing further.
Nothing makes me happy, nothing hurts me any more.

ANTIGONE I know. But I called you here for a reason:
to talk alone.

ISMENE I can see there's something important. Tell me.

21

ANTIGONE It's the burial. It's our brothers:
Kreon, honoring one and casting the other out.
They say he has buried Eteokles
with full and just and lawful honors due the dead;
but Polyneices, who died as pitiably—   30
Kreon has proclaimed that his body will stay unburied;
no mourners, no tomb, no tears,
a tasty meal for vultures.
That's what they say this man of good will
Kreon has proclaimed, for you, yes and for me;
and he is coming here to announce it
clearly, so that everyone will know.
And they say he intends to enforce it:
"Whoever shall perform any prohibited act
shall be liable to the penalty of death by stoning   40
in the presence of the assembled citizens."
You can see that you'll have to act quickly
to prove you are as brave today
as you were born to be.

ISMENE What can I accomplish? There's nothing left.
What can I do or undo?

ANTIGONE Will you join with me? Will you help?
Ask yourself that.

ISMENE Help with what?

ANTIGONE The body. Give me your hand. Help me.   50

ISMENE You mean to bury him? In spite of the edict?

ANTIGONE He's my brother and yours too;
and whether you will or not, I'll stand by him.

ISMENE Do you dare, despite Kreon?

ANTIGONE He cannot keep me from my own.

22

ISMENE Your own?
Think of Oedipus, our own father,
hated, infamous, destroyed;
found his crimes, broke his eyes,
that hand that murdered,   60
two in one—
and Mother, remember,
his mother and wife,
two in one,
her braids of rope that twisted life away—
then our brothers,
two in one day,
the hands that murdered
shared twin doom—
now us, sisters, two alone,   70
and all the easier destroyed
if we spite the law and the power of the king.

(No, we should be sensible:)
we are women, born unfit to battle men;
and we are subjects, while Kreon is king.
No, we must obey, even in this,
even if something could hurt more.
But because I will obey,
I beg forgiveness of the dead;
my plea is that I am forced;   80
to intervene would be senseless.

ANTIGONE Then I won't urge you. No,
Even if you were willing to "be senseless"
I wouldn't want the help you could give.
It's too late.
You must be as you believe.
I will bury him myself.
If I die for doing that, good:
I will stay with him, my brother;
and my crime will be devotion.   90
The living are here,

but I must please those longer
who are below; for with the dead
I will stay forever.
If you believe you must,
cast out these principles which the gods themselves honor.

ISMENE   I won't dishonor anything; but I cannot help,
not when the whole country refuses to help.

ANTIGONE   Then weakness will be your plea.
I am different. I love my brother   100
and I'm going to bury him, now.

ISMENE   Antigone, I'm so afraid for you.

ANTIGONE   Don't be afraid yet, not for me.
Steer your own fate. It's a long way.

ISMENE   Promise not to say anything.
Keep this secret. I'll join you in secrecy.

ANTIGONE   No, shout it, proclaim it.
I'll hate you the more for keeping silence.

ISMENE   Hate me?
This ardor of yours is spent on ashes.   110
Will is not enough.
There is no way, without power.

ANTIGONE   When my strength is spent, I will be done.
I know I am pleasing those whom I must.

ISMENE   With no hope, even to start is wrong.

ANTIGONE   Talk like that, and you'll make me hate you;
and he, dead, will hate you,
and rightly, as an enemy.

24

Leave me alone, with my hopeless scheme;
I'm ready to suffer for it and to die.   120
Let me. No suffering could be so terrible
as to die for nothing.

ISMENE   Since you believe you must, go on.
You are wrong. But we who love you
are right in loving you.

ANTIGONE *and* ISMENE *part,* ANTIGONE *to the left, the west,*
ISMENE *to the right. Bright daylight now pours from the*
right where the CHORUS *enters, fifteen white-bearded gentle-*
men, whose courtiers' garb, spangled with golden dragons
and sunbursts, reflects the color of new day. They about-face
toward the sun. They pray:

CHORUS   Sun-blaze, shining at last,
you are the most beautiful light
ever shown Thebes
over her seven gates;

and now, higher,   130
widening gaze of gold day,
you come,
over the course of our west river.

In whole armor,
come out of Argos
(his shield shone white)
you have expelled the man,
exiled in unbridled and blinding flight.

Out of the crisis of a dubious quarrel
Polyneices had roused him against our country   140
As shrill as an eagle on wings white as snow
he flew onto the country,
feathered in armor,

many men full-armed
and plumes on their helmets.

Stood there, over our roofs;
circled our gates, Thebes' seven faces;
spears, set for the kill,
snarling about the wall;

a gullet gaping,   150
dry for a fill of our blood;
fires
ready to catch our wreath of towers;

but then nothing.
Now he was gone,
fled the war god's crash,
snared in flight by the war god.
Futile to have struggled with dragon Thebes.

Zeus hates the noise of a bragging tongue.
When he saw them come against us   160
in a great gush, grandiose with splashing gold,
he whirled fire;
and the man who was rushing like a racer to the goal
on the heights of our battlements
and was signaling victory,
Zeus hurled him down with that fire.

Swung and then fell,
with the torch in his hand still,
on our land;
struck, and the land returned the shock.   170

He who had raved drunk, raged to attack,
who had howled with sweeps of the wind of hatred,
fell baffled;
and the grand war god allotted the rest their own dooms,
pressed as they failed,
gained us the contest.

Our seven gates were their seven stations,
and standing against our own, their seven captains,
who were turned by Zeus and ran
and to Zeus abandoned their bronze squadrons.   180
But on either side, one man remained, out of hatred,
seed of one father, birth from one mother,
planted spears against each other,
and both of them conquered,
sharing a twin death.

Victory comes
bringing glory to Thebes,
answers a smile
to our many chariots that cheer her.
Now that the war is over, forget war.   190
We'll visit every god's temples,
for a whole night, dancing and chanting praise.
Dionysos leads us,
rules Thebes,
makes the land tremble.

KORYPHAIOS   But look, the new king of the country,
Kreon, is coming:
a new kind of man for new conditions.
I wonder what program he intends to launch,
that he should call the elders into special conference.   200

> From the palace KREON enters, in armor, with a military
> retinue

KREON   Gentlemen, the state!
The gods have quaked her in heavy weather.
Now they have righted her.
The state rides steady once again.

Out of all the citizens, I have summoned you,
remembering that you blessed King Laios' reign;
when Oedipus ruled, you stood by him;

and after his destruction stood by his sons,
always with firm counsel.
Both sons died in one day, struck and stricken,   210
paired in doom and a twin pollution.
Now I rule, as next of kin.
They are dead; I am king.

It is impossible to know a man's soul,
both the wit and will,
before he writes laws and enforces them.
I believe that he who rules in a state
and fails to embrace the best men's counsels,
but stays locked in silence and vague fear,
is the worst man there.   220
I have long believed so.
And he who cherishes an individual beyond his homeland,
he, I say, is nothing.
Zeus who sees all will see I shall not stay silent
if I see disaster marching against our citizens,
and I shall not befriend the enemy of this land.
For the state is safety.
When she is steady, then we can steer.
Then we can love.

Those are my principles. The state will thrive through them.   230
Today I have proclaimed more laws akin to those.
These concern the sons of Oedipus:
Eteokles, who fought in defense of the nation
and fell in action,
will be given holy burial,
a funeral suited to greatness and nobility.
But his brother, Polyneices, the exile,
who descended with fire to destroy his fatherland and family
                gods,
to drink our blood and drive us off slaves,
will have no ritual, no mourners,   240
will be left unburied so men may see him
ripped for food by dogs and vultures.

This is an example of my thinking.
I shall never let criminals excel good men in honor.
I shall honor the friends of the state
while they live, and when they die.

KORYPHAIOS These opinions, sir,
concerning enemies and friends of the state,
are as you please.
Law and usage, as I see it,   250
are totally at your disposal
to apply both to the dead and to us survivors.

KREON Think of yourselves, therefore,
as the guardians of my pronouncements.

KORYPHAIOS You have young men you can put on duty.

KREON No, no! Not the corpse. I have guards posted.

KORYPHAIOS Then what are your orders?

KREON Not to side with rebels.

KORYPHAIOS No one is such a fool. No one loves death.

KREON That's right, death is the price.   260
All the same, time after time,
greed has destroyed good men.

                                    A SENTRY runs in from the left.

SENTRY King Kreon,
I'm going to
explain about
why I made it
down here all out of wind,
which for one thing
is not on account of going
fast,   270
because even when I started out

29

it wasn't light-footed.
No, and I kept stopping to think,
and all the way I was going in circles
about turning right back.
Yes, and my soul keeps telling me things.
Says: What are you going to go there for,
when as soon as you get there you're sure to pay for it?
And then: What are you standing here for?
If Kreon finds out about this from somebody else first   280
you'll be the one that suffers.
I kept rolling that over in my mind,
and moved along slow,
like on my own time:
you can go a long way, walking a short distance.
In the end the thought
that actually did win out
was to go right ahead to you, sir.
And even if what I'm about to explain
really isn't anything,   290
I'm going to say it anyhow,
because here I am,
yes, and with a handful of hope
that nothing more will happen to me
but what the future has in store already.

KREON What's the matter with you? What are you afraid of?

SENTRY Well, first I want to tell you about me,
        because I didn't do it, and don't know who did,
        so it wouldn't be right either way
        if I fell into some kind of trouble.   300

KREON You aim well before you shoot.
       You virtually encircle the business, you build a blockade.
       Clearly your news is extraordinary.

SENTRY Sir, it's awful; it was so strange
        I can hardly bring myself to say it.

KREON Tell me now,
then I'll dismiss you,
and you'll go.

SENTRY Well, I *am* telling you:
somebody up and buried the corpse and went off: 310
sprinkled dust over it
and did the ceremonies you're supposed to.

KREON Who? Who dared?

SENTRY I don't know.
There wasn't any cut from a pickax or scoop of a hoe.
The soil is hard and dry,
no breaks in it from wagon wheels.
No, whoever the one who did it was,
there's no sign of him now. Nothing at all.
When the first daytime sentry showed us   320
we all thought it was a miracle.
We couldn't see the body; and he wasn't really buried;
it was like someone tried to drive the curse out:
a fine dust on it.
No game tracks or dog tracks,
no sign of being tugged at.

Next thing there's a flurry of harsh words,
with one sentry cross-examining the other;
and we'd have wound up fighting,
with nobody there to stop us, either,   330
because everybody did it, and no one saw him do it,
and everyone testified he knew nothing about it.
We were ready to hold hot iron, walk through fire,
swearing by the gods we didn't do it
and never knew who did or planned it, either one.

But in the end, when we'd tried everything,
one man speaks up
and sets us all hanging our heads

looking at the ground afraid,
because we couldn't say a thing against it   340
and couldn't expect good to come of doing it.
He said we couldn't hide what happened,
we had to tell you.
And that idea won out.
With my bad luck, the lot fell on me,
and I'm the winner, and here I am,
and I don't want to be
and I know you don't want me here
because no one who hates what you say loves you.

KORYPHAIOS My lord, we have been considering   350
whether a god might not have done this. . . .

KREON Stop, before you say too much.
You're an old man. Are you senile?
Intolerable talk,
as if gods had any concern for that corpse,
covering him up,
honoring him presumably as a public benefactor,
when he was the one who came to burn their temples,
the circles of pillars and the holy treasures
and the country that is theirs,   360
smashing the laws.
Is that your idea?
Can you see gods honoring criminals?
Impossible.

No. For a long while now
certain men in this city, as they would have it,
have scarcely been able to stand up under my commands.
They mutter about me, they hide, shake their heads
instead of properly shouldering the yoke and working with
              the team,
which is the one way of showing love to me.   370
Those are the men that did this, I'm positive.
They were seduced with money.

Money: nothing worse for people
ever has sprouted up and grown current.
That's what ravages nations and drives men from their homes,
perverts the best human principles,
teaches men to turn to crime,
makes everything they do and think unholy.

Everyone they hired to do this will pay for it.
As Zeus accepts my prayers,   380
understand this well, I'm talking on oath,
to you (*to* SENTRY)
unless you find me the perpetrator of this burial
death won't be enough,
you'll hang alive till you tell me who did it,
just so you'll, all of you, know from then on
not to take bribes, and learn that your love
of getting what you can where you can is wrong.
You'll see: When you have it, shame makes you hide it;
that kind of money wrecks men,   390
and few escape alive.

SENTRY   Will you give me a chance to answer,
                    or should I just go?

KREON   Don't you know yet your talk irritates me?

SENTRY   Does it hurt in your ears, sir, or in your soul?

KREON   What is this? Anatomy?

SENTRY   The man who did it irritates your mind.
            I just bother your ears.

KREON   You can't stop talking, can you?
            You must have been born this way.   400

SENTRY   Anyway, I never did what you said I did.

KREON Yes you did! For money! You sold your soul.

SENTRY Sir, it's terrible; you make your mind up
        when even what's wrong looks right.

KREON I'll leave the subtleties to you. I make decisions.
        But unless you show me the responsible parties in this case
        you will learn that easy money buys suffering.

                                        Re-enters the palace.

SENTRY I hope they find him.
        But if he's caught or if he's not,
        which is something luck will decide,   410
        you won't ever see me come back here.
        No, because I never thought or hoped even,
        but, thanks to the gods and praise them, I'm alive.

                                        Exit, to the east.

CHORUS Many marvels walk through the world,
        terrible, wonderful,
        but none more than humanity,
        which makes a way under winter rain,
        over the gray deep of the sea,
        proceeds where it swells and swallows;
        that grinds at the Earth—   420
        undwindling, unwearied, first of the gods—
        to its own purpose,
        as the plow is driven, turning year into year,
        through generations as colt follows mare.

        Weaves and braids the nets meshes to hurl—
        circumspect man—
        and to drive lightheaded tribes of birds his prisoners,
        and the animals,
        nations in fields, race of the salty ocean;
        and fools and conquers the monsters   430
        whose roads and houses are hills,

34

the shaggy-necked horse that he holds subject,
and the mountain oxen that he yokes under beams,
bowing their heads,
his unwearying team.

The breath of his life he has taught to be
language, be the spirit of thought;
griefs, to give laws to nations;
fears, to dodge weapons
of rains and winds and the homeless cold—   440
always clever,
he never fails to find ways
for whatever future;
manages cures for the hardest maladies;
from death alone he has secured no refuge.

With learning and with ingenuity
over his horizon of faith
mankind crawls
now to failure, now to worth.
And when he has bound the laws of this earth   450
beside Justice pledged to the gods,
he rules his homeland;
but he has no home
7. Anhgone who recklessly marries an illegitimate cause.
Fend this stranger from my mind's and home's hearth.

KORYPHAIOS An unholy miracle. Am I right or mistaken?
How can I say no,
this is not the girl that I know,
Antigone?

From the right, the SENTRY *leads* ANTIGONE *forward.*

Daughter of Oedipus,   460
not you? Where is he taking you?
You haven't broken the laws of the king,

have you? That would be senseless.
Why have they arrested you?

SENTRY   This girl here is the one who buried him.
We caught her at it. Where's Kreon?

KORYPHAIOS   There he is, leaving the palace.
He's coming back just when we need him.

> KREON *returns. He is now in regalia, and has a retinue of*
> *armed slaves.*

KREON   To come forward just in time
seems to be my fate.   470
How do you need me?

SENTRY   King Kreon,
there's nothing a man can swear won't happen.
What you think later makes you wrong before.
I could have sworn I'd never come here again.
The way you threatened me shook me like a storm.
But happiness you never hope for
makes every other joy look smaller.
Here I am, though I swore an oath I'd never come,
bringing this girl we caught tidying the grave up.
This time I wasn't picked by lot,   480
no, this is a lucky find that's mine and nobody else's.
Yes, and here she is, she's yours:
take her and cross-examine her and judge her, just as you
                please.
And as for me, I'm free now, and rightly so,
and rid of this trouble.

KREON   This girl? Where did you find her? And how?

SENTRY   She's the one that buried that man.
Now you know all I know.

36

KREON   Are you sure you're saying what you mean?

SENTRY This is the girl I saw   490
        bury that dead man you said not to.
        That's what I'm telling you, plain and clear.

KREON   How did you spot her? How did you stop her and arrest her?

SENTRY It was like this.
        When we got back from you with those terrible threats on us,
        we swept off all the dust that covered the corpse up,
        stripped it naked;
        the body was oozing,
        and we sat down on a hilltop between the wind and it
        to dodge the smell,   500
        one man busy shaking the next man, with harsh words
                rushing
        so nobody could be lazy on the job this time.

        This went on all the while
        till the sun was a glittering circle
        that stood in the middle of the air
        and warmed and then seared.
        And suddenly a whirlwind, like a smudge fire,
        raised a squall off the soil and trouble in heaven;
        and it filled the plain,
        and tortured the leaves of the woods in the level places,   510
        and forced the mighty air full.
        We squinted and suffered out this holy misery.
        After a long time, it was sent away.
        Then we saw the girl.

        She wailed out loud:
        that sharp sound out of bitterness
        a bird makes when she looks in her nest and it's empty,
        it's a widow's bed and the baby chicks are gone.
        And this girl,

when she saw the corpse was bare,   520
she cried that same way and groaned and mourned for it,
and she prayed hard curses on the one who did that to it.
Right away she brings dust, handful by handful,
then pours offerings three times,
holding a beautiful urn up high
like for giving a crown.

We watched that,
then quick as a shot hunted her down,
and right off got her, not a bit afraid.
We accused her of doing it before and this time, both,   530
and she didn't deny a thing,
which made me glad and sad at the same time.
I've cleared myself and arrested her:
When you go free, nothing makes you happier;
and when you hurt someone you care about,
                    nothing can hurt more.
But I'm naturally the kind of man
that puts everything second to his own safety.

KREON (*to* ANTIGONE) You now,
you hanging your head, looking at the ground,
do you admit or deny you did this?   540

ANTIGONE I did it. I deny nothing.

KREON (*to* SENTRY) As for you,
you may convey your person wherever you wish.
This is a grave charge; and you are free of it.

                                        Exit SENTRY.

(*To* ANTIGONE) Now tell me, briefly and concisely:
were you aware of the proclamation prohibiting those acts?

ANTIGONE I was.
I couldn't avoid it when it was made public.

KREON You still dared break this law?

ANTIGONE Yes, because I did not believe   550
that Zeus was the one who had proclaimed it;
neither did Justice,
or the gods of the dead whom Justice lives among.
The laws they have made for men are well marked out.
I didn't suppose your decree had strength enough,
or you, who are human,
to violate the lawful traditions
the gods have not written merely, but made infallible.
These laws are not for now or for yesterday,
they are alive forever;   560
and no one knows when they were shown to us first.
I did not intend to pay, before the gods,
for breaking these laws
because of my fear of one man and his principles.
I was thoroughly aware I would die
before you proclaimed it;
of course I would die, even if you hadn't.
Since I will die, and early, I call this profit.
Anyone who lives the troubled life I do
must benefit from death.   570

No, I do not suffer from the fact of death.
But if I had let my own brother stay unburied
I would have suffered all the pain I do not feel now.
And if you decide what I did was foolish,
you may be fool enough to convict me too.

KORYPHAIOS Clearly she's her father's child, hard and raw.
He never learned to yield, for all his troubles.

KREON Yes, but these stiff minds are the first to collapse.
Fire-tempered iron, the strongest and toughest,
that's the kind you most often see snapped and shattered.   580
I know horses:
slim reins discipline even the spirited ones.

You can't be brave and free with your master near by.

Laws were made. She broke them.
Rebellion to think of it,
then to do it and do it again,
now more defiance, bragging about it,
she did it and she's laughing.
I'm no man—
she is a man, she's the king—   590
if she gets away with this.
My niece, or let her be
closer than any who pray at my home hearth,
she and her kin cannot prevent their doom.
Yes, the other girl, I hold her
equally responsible for plotting the burial.
Summon her immediately.

                              An armed slave goes to the palace.

Just now I saw her at home, hysterical,
out of her wits. A thieving mind
scheming crooked plans in its own darkness   600
loves to be caught before it can act.
But what I really hate is the one
that, once it's caught, wants to beautify its guilt.

ANTIGONE You have caught me. What more do you want?
          Isn't killing me enough?

KREON I want? No. With that I have everything.

ANTIGONE Then why are you waiting?
          There is nothing you can say I would like to hear,
          and there never could be.
          And obviously there is nothing about me   610
          that could please you either.

          Still, where was there a way for me
          to win greater fame or glory

than by simply taking my own brother to his grave?
There should be a voice among these gentlemen
to say I have pleased them too;
but all have been locked in silence by fear.
A king may do and say what he wishes.
This is his greatest good fortune.

KREON You're the only citizen who holds that view.   620
The rest are with me. Aren't you ashamed
to dissent from these good men?

ANTIGONE No, they keep silent to please you.
Why should I be ashamed of loyalty to my brother?

KREON Wasn't his enemy your brother?
Why do you honor Polyneices only?
Isn't that the same as rejecting Eteokles?

ANTIGONE Yes, they were brothers, one blood,
father and mother, the same as mine.
Eteokles is dead: he will not say I have rejected him.   630

KREON He will if you honor him no more than Polyneices,
who died ravaging this land, while he defended it.

ANTIGONE He's not his slave, but his brother;
and he's dead. And Death is a god
who wants his laws obeyed.

KREON Not that good and bad be treated
equally under those laws.

ANTIGONE Does anyone know?
Maybe, down there, all this is pure. → No greek heaven.
↳ Both I (Antigone) & You (Kreon) may be right.

KREON Enemies and friends are two different things,   640
and dying doesn't reconcile them.

ANTIGONE And I wasn't born to hate one with the other,
          but to love both together.

KREON If you must love somebody
       go down there and love the dead.
       I'm alive though, and no woman will rule me.

                              ISMENE *enters from the palace, under arrest.*

CHORUS (*severally*) Here, Antigone, is your sister. . . . She loves
        you. . . .

        She is weeping. . . . She blushes . . . a lovely face . . .

        when clouds on its brow wet a mountain's cheek
        which the sky has painted with blood. . . .   650

KREON (*to* ISMENE) You, in my own home,
       slunk like a viper, sneaking, sucked my blood,
       and I never learned I was nursing a pair of traitors:
       but now, tell me,
       say you shared in this burial
       or swear you knew nothing about it.

ISMENE I did it. If she is with me now,
        I share the blame with her and will bear it also.

ANTIGONE No, you have no right. You weren't willing to,
          and even if you had been I wouldn't have taken you with me.   660

ISMENE Now that you're in trouble
        I'm not afraid to weather suffering with you.
        I have made myself ready.

ANTIGONE The god of death and the dead are my witnesses
          to who did what. I do not want love
          from anyone who loves with speeches.

ISMENE Please don't, you're my sister;
        don't take away from me the honor of dying with you,
        and of joining with you in service to the dead.

ANTIGONE You will not die, not with me you won't.   670
        You had nothing to do with this; don't try to claim you had.
        I will die, and the dead be served well.

ISMENE What is life when I've lost you?
        What is there to love in life?

ANTIGONE Ask your uncle Kreon.
        You have so much in common.

ISMENE Why should you hurt me? It doesn't help.

ANTIGONE Hurt you? Maybe I am laughing at you.
        If I am laughing, it's out of sorrow.

ISMENE Then what can I still do to help you?   680

ANTICONE Save yourself. I want you to escape.

ISMENE No, please, don't make me let you die alone.

ANTIGONE You chose to live. I chose to die.

ISMENE I tried: I argued.

ANTIGONE You argued well, and I did;
        and to those who agree with each,
        each of us was right.

ISMENE But now we both share the blame, right or wrong.

ANTIGONE Be happy. You are living;   690
        but my soul died long ago, to be useful among the dead.

43

KREON (*to* ISMENE) Two girls: one born that way,
and now you turn out to be a fool too.

ISMENE A mind does not just grow and then stand.
When our lives founder reason deserts us.

KREON Yes, minds like yours and hers;
when you commit crimes you wreck your lives.

ISMENE What is there left for me alone?
Without her how can I live?

KREON Forget her. She no longer exists.   700

ISMENE Do you mean you will kill the girl
you promised your own son would marry?

KREON There are other fields for him to furrow.

ISMENE But for him and her no other match like this.

KREON There is no match when the wife is worthless.

ISMENE It's Haimon you cast aside when you say that.
Don't you love your son? Can you deprive him?

KREON No. Death will stop that wedding.
And this is the end:
I'm sick of you and this marriage business.   710

KORYPHAIOS It has been determined, then,
that Antigone shall die?

KREON Yes, and you as well as I have determined it.
Stop wasting time. Hurry,
take them both inside.
Now they'll have to be women and know their place.

44

Even men, rash men, run
when they see how close death is to life.

ANTIGONE *and* ISMENE *are led into the palace.* KREON
follows.

CHORUS Lucky those whose lifetime knows no taste of trouble.
The house quaked by the gods   720
lacks no form of disaster
creeping after all the clan;
like swellings of ocean,
when evil north winds breathe,
that run on the abyss of brine
and roll black sand up from the chasm—
and headlands beat them back
but bellow, wailing, wind-worn.

I can see the ancient griefs of dead men striking
this house, ripped by some god,   730
no relief, generation after generation,
no release.
But the spreading last light,
the last root, stock of Oedipus,
is now hacked down,
with blood-red dust up from the nether gods,
madness made of logic,
principle turned frenzy.

KREON *returns.*

Could man pass,
and could man keep the force down that is yours, Zeus?   740
Which not sleep which traps all,
nor the months, as undwindling as gods, can stop?
Within time, but without age,
through force you keep
the twinkle and blaze of Olympos yours.
And for next, and for soon as for then,
this one law will hold man in:

that no greatness creeps down
into the life destined to death
without bringing disaster.   750

Though stray hope
out of light-headed longing is a help many need,
others find hope a disastrous deception
that creeps on fools
who step into the blaze.
It was someone wise
who made the illustrious dictum known:—
When a god drives him, and deceives,
a man will decide
what is bad is good,   760
and lives only a brief while
outside disaster.

                              HAIMON enters, from the palace.

KORYPHAIOS But here is Haimon: you have no other son.
            Has he come out of grief, Kreon,
            for the fate of Antigone,
            or in the pain of his own loss?

KREON We'll soon see; and seeing is better than prophecy.
       Son, have you heard the final verdict?
       Are you angry at your father,
       or do you love me regardless,   770
       whatever I do and how?

HAIMON I am your son.
        You direct a course for me with good intentions,
        and I follow it.
        I don't believe marriage is more important to me
        than you and your good leadership.

KREON Son, you should hold that to your heart.
       Everything is second to a father's will.

That's the reason men pray for children,
to have them growing up at home,   780
boys, obedient,
the kind to punish those who hate their father
and honor those who love him
as much as he does himself.
The man who has worthless children—
what has he got for himself but hardship
and a laugh for his enemies?

That's how things are.
Don't throw out principle for a little fun,
for the sake of a woman.   790
Remember a treacherous wife turns cold in your arms,
and no one can hurt you worse than a false friend.
Kick this out of your system.
Send that girl off like any other enemy.
Let her be a bride in Hades' household.

I caught her in open rebellion,
her alone out of all the nation.
I won't be a leader who lies to his people.
No: I will kill her.
Let her sing a song to Zeus for the bonds of blood.   800
If I rear a disorderly family
I am feeding general disorder.

Anyone who's a good man inside his house
is a just man where the state is concerned.
Any man who breaks laws,
uses violence against them,
thinks he can give orders to stronger men,
gains no praise from me.

The state: when she sets someone up, you must obey him
in small matters, in just acts, and in both opposites.   810
For my part, I am confident
that a man willing to be ruled can himself rule well.

He is the one who stands firm in the storm of battle,
holds his post in front of you and by your side,
rightly, nobly.

Nothing is worse than lack of leadership.
It destroys nations, drives men from their homes,
smashes armies, makes allies defect.
But when men are ruled right
their obedience to authority saves their lives.   820

That's why we have to defend orderly people,
and never let women get the better of us.
If we must fall, better to fall to a real man
and not be called worse than women.

KORYPHAIOS In my belief,
            unless time has robbed me of discernment,
            you are speaking intelligently on this subject.

HAIMON Father, the gods implant intelligence in humans.
        Of all our properties, that is the supreme one.
        I lack the power and the training to tell you you're wrong,   830
        and that's just as well.
        But perhaps a second opinion will be valuable.

        I am bound naturally
        to watch over anything concerning you:
        what people say or do
        or what fault anyone can find with you.
        Because, for the common man, your gaze is terrible.
        He can't find words to explain things that displease you.
        But I do hear things, under cover of darkness,
        what our country says, in grief for this girl: 840

        that no one is more innocent,
        no death more awful,
        no deeds more noble than hers;
        with her own brother fallen slaughtered,

then not buried,
she wouldn't leave him for dogs' and crows' butchering.
Shouldn't her fate be golden glory?
Isn't she worthy?

That is the word.
It is dark, and marches in silence.   850

There is no possession, Father, that I honor more
than your happiness and fortune.
After all, what greater prize can children possess
than a father flourishing in glory
and glorying in their honor?

Please, be different this once.
Believe in what someone else says for once.
Whenever a man supposes that he alone
has intelligence or expression or feelings,
he exposes himself and shows his emptiness.   860
But it's no shame even for a wise man
to learn and to relent.

In the winter floods you can see
how the trees that give way save every stem,
and how those that strain are destroyed, uprooted.
In the same way, the man who tightens the halyard
and doesn't slacken it, is capsized.

Don't be angry. Allow yourself some leeway.
Let me give my opinion, young as I am:—
It would be best if we were born knowing everything;   870
but it is honorable to learn from honest men.

KORYPHAIOS What he says is to the point, sir.
You may do well to learn from him. And you too, from your
              father.
Both have spoken well.

KREON Men our age, learn from him?

HAIMON If I happen to be right? Suppose I am young.
Don't look at my age, look at what I do.

KREON What you do? Give your loyalty to rebels?

HAIMON No, nor would I ever encourage anyone else
to respect or be faithful to someone who is doing wrong.   880

KREON But didn't that girl do wrong?

HAIMON The whole nation denies it.

KREON Will the nation tell me what orders I can give?

HAIMON See? You're talking like a boy.

KREON It's my job to rule this land.
There is no one else.

HAIMON No country belongs to one man.

KREON Nations belong to the men with power.
That's common knowledge.

HAIMON You could rule a desert right,   890
if you were alone there.

KREON Look at him! Taken that woman's side, fighting me.

HAIMON I'm on your side. It's you I'm concerned about.

KREON A fine son you are, putting me on the stand.

HAIMON It's because I can see you're making a mistake.
You're a witness against yourself.

KREON What mistake? Respecting my high office?

HAIMON Respecting it? By dishonoring the gods?

KREON Rotten, degraded, on your knees to a woman!
Everything you've said was for her sake.   900

HAIMON And for my sake, and yours especially,
and for the nether gods as well.
You can tell me I'm on my knees,
but you will find that I never surrender
when I know something is wrong.

KREON There's no use.
You'll never marry Antigone. Not in this world.

HAIMON Then she'll die, and her death will destroy others.

KREON Are you threatening me?

HAIMON No, I'm arguing, in a void.   910

KREON Of your own mind; and trying to teach me.
Your tears will teach you.

HAIMON If you weren't my father, I'd say you'd lost your mind.

KREON Don't "father" me. You're no man. You're a slave.
Property of a woman.

HAIMON And you expect to talk but not listen,
and to speak but not be judged by what you say.

KREON Just understand:
You don't insult me and go off laughing.
Bring her here! Let him see her.   920
Kill her here, beside her bridegroom.

51

HAIMON No, you won't. Don't think it.
        While I am with her, she will not die.
        And you, you will never see me again.
        Stay with your friends, if these are friends,
        and rave at them, if they'll listen.

                              Rushes out, to the left.

KORYPHAIOS Sir, it was anger that made him run away.
            When a person his age is hurt, he can be dangerous.

KREON Let him try, let him imagine; he's only a man.
       He can't save those two girls.   930

KORYPHAIOS Two girls? Do you plan to kill both?

KREON No. You're right: Ismene didn't help her. Thank you.

KORYPHAIOS Antigone, then. By what form of execution?

KREON Have her taken up a road men have deserted;
       hidden there, living, in a rock hollow;
       leave her enough fodder only
       to defend the country from the filth of a curse.
       There she can beg from Death, the only god she honors;
       possibly Death will excuse her from dying!
       That, or she'll learn, too late,   940
       that homage to Death and the dead is useless.

              KREON *returns to the palace. Now it is noon. The harsh sun*
                                    stands in the square.

CHORUS Desire, you, unconquered in war;
        Desire, vaulting upon our dear goods;
        at night you rest on young girls' gentle smiles,
        then travel, grazing the deep ocean,
        to visit the far dwellers whose houses are fields.
        The deathless gods cannot escape,

52

or humans whose whole life is a day.
Welcoming you, they run mad.

You twist good and just men to crime and shame.   950
You shook the rift in one blood,
revolt among these men.
Clear longing in the lowered eyes of a young bride
is your victory.
Your power is equal, your place beside
the great gods and eternal mandates;
for Love conquers without war, and destroys with glad games.

KORYPHAIOS Now, though, even I am borne
outside those mandates laid down for here
when I see, there . . .   960

ANTIGONE *is led from the palace by armed slaves.*

and I cannot dam the force of my tears
when I see Antigone
who is reaching the end of her progress
to the room and the bed of universal rest.

ANTIGONE Look at me now, citizens of my homeland.
I walk the last path
watching my last of sunlight. Never again,
for Death, giver of universal rest,
is taking me, living, to the shore of the river of Pain.
No wedding song has been sung for this bride.   970
I have lost that birthright.

CHORUS You go with fame and in glory
to the hidden place of the dead.
No sickness has diminished you:
no weapon has paid you war's wages.
You descend to the kingdom of Death
alive, of your own accord,
you alone of mortal women.

ANTIGONE Niobe, a stranger, once queen of our country,
          I know of her death: 980
          like tightened ivy a stone growth covered her.
          Now she shrinks in incessant rain and snowfall,
          and off her brow, a cliff,
          fall tears to drench the hill breast.
          Mine is like her death night.

CHORUS   But she was a god, descendant of a god,
          and we are human and born to die.
          Still, your doom is worth grand fame;
          for living and dying, both, you share
          the heritage of the gods' equals.   990

ANTIGONE No, no: laughing at me!
          Can't you wait till I'm gone to insult me?
          Home, country, my city,
          citizens, you, men grand in possessions,
          west river, holy plain of Thebes splendid with chariots,
          now I have made you all my witnesses:
          how, friendless, unmourned, I go to what strange funeral
          and under what kind of law.
          Wait to laugh. I have been unlucky.
          I come as a stranger always to the home hearth   1000
          of humans and spirits both,
          an alien only, among the living and the dead.

CHORUS   You were harsh and daring, child.
          You went too far and fell broken
          against the lofty pedestal of Justice.
          Perhaps, though, you are paying
          for some ancestral failing.

ANTIGONE The memory that wounds most,
          turned like plowland year to year:
          my father's griefs, the family   1010
          doomed whole in its glory, disastrous deceptions,
          the bed incest lay in, mother and father,

condemned men—these are my origins.
There: you opened that wound again, not I.
So condemned, I will find a new place,
not a home, a spinster's residence, with them,
with Polyneices—doomed young by alliance,
marriage in Argos, exile from our home—
by whose death I died and still lived.

CHORUS Your devotion is a kind of reverence.   1020
Power, though, must be revered, not trampled
by those who must wield it.

                                          KREON *enters.*

But you, holding rebellion,
followed your own destruction.

ANTIGONE Unmourned, friendless, I am led away.
The path is ready. They sing no wedding song.
I will never be able to see—there!
the holy eye of radiant day—again.
But my fate is my own, to die;
and there is no one I love who sighs over me.   1030

KREON Singing and sighing!
If it were any use to talk before you die
no one would ever stop.
Take her away. Hurry!
Shut the tomb where it arches over, the way I told you;
leave her there, alone. Either she'll die,
or, if she likes her new house, she can live in it, buried.
Our hands are clean.
She was only a stranger in our world,
and her stay is over.   1040

ANTIGONE To my tomb, my wedding, my home
the eternal vigil of the grave:
I am going to my own people there,

where Persephone has welcomed their greater number
among the spirits of the dead.
I am the last and least.
Before my time, I am descending to that world;
but I am returning home as well, from an exile.

As I go, I nurse the hope in my heart
that you, Father and Mother, will love me and be with me,   1050
and you, brother, will let me see your face.
When you died, it was I, with my own hands,
who bathed you and tidied you, both of you,
and who gave offerings at your graveside.
Polyneices, I buried you too.
And today, this is my reward.

But I was right to honor you,
and men who understand will agree.
Suppose I had been a mother and widow.
I would not have taken this burden on   1060
or defied the nation, in that case.
The principle I followed is this:
If my husband had died, there might be another,
and a son by another man if I had lost my children.
But my mother and father were gone.
I could never have had a new brother.

It was on that principle, Polyneices,
        I honored you above all.
To Kreon it seemed wrong, a terrible act of daring.
He had me caught and held,   1070
and today he is taking me living to the grave.
And I never was loved,
I never nursed a child;
and with those I love gone,
I go alone and desolate.

What divine and just law have I evaded?
Is there any use in my looking toward the gods?

Is there any ally among the gods I can call to,
if my reverence has made me impious?
But if this is the will of the gods,   1080
we will learn we were wrong through suffering.
But if these others are wrong,
I can pray for nothing worse for them
than what they are doing to me,
their unjust justice.

KORYPHAIOS   The same torrents of the soul
still compel this girl.

KREON   I said to take her out. Guards!
No more delay, or you'll suffer for it.

ANTIGONE   In your words, death is approaching.   1090

KREON   I won't encourage you. You've been condemned.

ANTIGONE   Land of Thebes, city of my fathers,
ancient gods of Thebes,
I can wait no longer.
You, the nation's leaders, look
at the last daughter of the house of your kings,
and see what I suffer at my mother's brother's hands
for an act of loyalty and devotion.

*Slaves lead her out to the left, the west. Now the sun begins
to follow.*

CHORUS   Danaë suffered the same fate,
exchanging the sky's heavenly light   1100
for locked halls fastened with brass.
Hidden within a tomb that became her marriage
                        chamber
she was yoked down, head bowed under.
Nevertheless, this proud child of a glorious race
received and stored the Golden Rain;

the seed of Zeus was her treasure.
But the force of fate is terrible,
inescapable,
riches and war, strong cities and sea-beaten ships notwith-
        standing.

And he, king and a king's son,   1110
Lykurgos, was yoked, fastened in stone.
And there, that terrible mood,
flourishing madness, trickled away; and he, the scoffer,
who had touched truth with his laughter,
now understood that this same Dionysos was god,
and had imprisoned him because
he tried suppressing the fervor
of the faithful, fire of holiness,
and had then no less
angered the Muses, lovers of ritual beat danced to piping.   1120

By the black cliffs where the broad sea is cleft
are the headlands of Thrace and the beach of the Bosporus,
where once the god of war, a neighbor there, watched
while the twin sons of Phineus were blinded
by their father's wife:
the damning wound and the unforgiving eyes,
savage hands and weapons bloodied.

As they fell, hopeless, they wept hopeless pain,
and their mother, divorced and imprisoned.
But she was from an ancient house and daughter of the
        North Wind;   1130
and in far caves, among her father's hurricanes,
was nursed and healed.
Now, flying even, or riding hills,
she knew well how harshly fate oppressed her.

TEIRESIAS *enters from the east. The declining sun is full in*
his face, but he proceeds unblinking. He is terribly old. A
                                boy leads him by the hand.

TEIRESIAS Nobles of Thebes,
we two have come one common path,
one man watching the way for both.
The blind must walk where others lead.

KREON Dear old Teiresias! But is there something wrong?

TEIRESIAS I will inform you. That is my prophetic duty.   1140
Yours is to comply.

KREON I have never disobeyed you in the past . . .

TEIRESIAS In consequence, you've been a good captain for the state,
and steered her right.

KREON . . . and I can attest, from my experience,
to the utility . . .

TEIRESIAS Then listen, please:
Once more you are walking the razor's edge.

KREON What do you mean?

TEIRESIAS You will know when you hear what the signs are: 1150

Seated at my station of augury,
a harbor under my command since ancient days,
where every bird puts in in safety,
I heard weird cries:
birds squawking in an evil frenzy.
They were tearing one another, clawing for murder.
The whirring of their wings made this clear.
It frightened me.
Immediately I lit the altars for sacrifice.
I tried; but, from the offerings,   1160
no flash.
Instead, a putrid slime dribbled down
and smoked and spat in the ashes.

The gall exploded in vapor.
The fat peeled off the thighs, exposing them,
the bones slithering.
The ritual had failed.

All that, I learned from this boy.
He guides me, as I do others.

The state is sick.   1170
You and your principles are to blame.
Every altar and hearth has been loaded
with fodder brought by birds and dogs off him,
the fallen son of Oedipus.
Therefore, the gods reject our prayers and our sacrifices,
and birds, feeding fat on a murdered man's blood,
scream nonsense.

My son,
stop and consider.
All mankind is subject to error.   1180
Once a mistake is made, and a man stumbles into
            misfortune,
it is both wise and worthy of him
to make amends and not be unbending.
Stubbornness is stupidity. It is criminal.
No. Give yourself leeway. Yield.
When someone has been destroyed, do you stab him?
            Give in.
What good is it to kill the dead again?
What kind of power is it?

I have spoken frankly for your own good.
When you benefit from what he tells you   1190
it is a true pleasure
to learn from an honest man.

KREON Old man,
all of you shoot at me like archers at a bull's-eye.
No, this fortune-telling isn't new to me.

You and your kind, for a long time now,
have been selling me out and trying to deliver me.

Make money!
Deal in silvered gold from Sardis, get gold from India:
that's what you want.   1200
But bury that man, no!
No, not if the eagles rip him for food,
not if they carry him to the throne of Zeus!
I'm not afraid even of that. I won't let you bury him.
I know full well no man has the power to pollute gods.
But you, my dear Teiresias, old as you are, listen:
It's you wonderfully clever people that fall hardest in disgrace
when you hide ugly ideas in pretty speeches
in order to make money.

TEIRESIAS Doesn't anyone know, won't anyone consider . . .   1210

    KREON Consider what?
           What universal truth are you going to proclaim?

TEIRESIAS . . . how much more valuable than money
           good advice is?

    KREON Or how much worse losing your judgment is?

TEIRESIAS And that is what's wrong with you.
           You are a sick man.

    KREON I don't choose to return the insult.
           You're supposed to be a prophet.

TEIRESIAS But you're doing just that.   1220
           You say my prophecies are lies.

    KREON Yes, and I say so because you love cash,
           all of you, prophetic profiteers. . . .

TEIRESIAS And tyrants love to have their own way
           regardless of right and wrong.

KREON Do you know who you're talking to?
       We're your rulers.

TEIRESIAS I know you are. It's thanks to me
           that you saved the state and rule now.

KREON Thanks to your skill as a prophet.   1230
       But as a man, you don't care about right or wrong.

TEIRESIAS And you are forcing me to tell you things I know
           and would prefer to leave undisturbed.

KREON Go ahead, disturb them, tell me.
       But don't expect to benefit by it.

TEIRESIAS I don't expect that you will.

KREON Just understand: I'm not for sale.
       I have principles.

TEIRESIAS Very well. Now you understand this:

           Few courses of the racing sun remain   1240
           before you lose a child of your own loins
           and give him back, a corpse, exchange for corpses.
           You have dishonored a living soul with exile in the tomb,
           hurling a member of this upper world below.
           You are detaining here, moreover,
           a dead body, unsanctified, and so unholy,
           a subject of the nether gods.

           The matter is out of your hands and those of the gods above.
           A crime of violence is being done and you are commanding it.
           Therefore, relentless destroyers pursue you,   1250
           Furies of death and deity;

62

they lie in wait for you now
to catch you in the midst of your crimes.

Consider that, and see if I've been bribed.
The time is near.
Weeping of women and men will be heard in your house.
All the enemy nations will be aroused,
all whose altars are stinking and corrupted
with the torn fragments the dogs, wild beasts, and birds
       bring.

You have hurt me. These facts   1260
are the arrows that I fire into your heart,
unfailing, like a marksman.
You will not escape their pain by running.

Boy, lead me home.
Kreon can fire on younger men.
He ought to teach his tongue silence
and his mind better principles.

               The boy leads TEIRESIAS *away.*

KORYPHAIOS Kreon, I've lived a long time,
         and I, no, none of us
         has ever known Teiresias to lie.   1270

KREON I know it. I know. I'm not sure any more.
      It's terrible to give in. What can I do?
      Resist? I may be deluding myself.

KORYPHAIOS You need prudent council, sir.

KREON What should I do? Tell me. I promise to comply.

KORYPHAIOS Go, release the girl from the cave.
         and build a tomb for the body you cast out.

KREON   That's your advice? To give in?

KORYPHAIOS   As quickly as possible.
             The gods are swift to strike.   1280
             They cut fools' hesitations short.

KREON   Oh, it's hard. This is not what I hoped.
             I'll do as you say. I must not fight
             wrongly, only to be defeated, against fate.

KORYPHAIOS   Then act now. Go. Don't leave it to others.

KREON   I will, at once.
             Attendants! Here! Some of you call the rest. Here!
             You, hurry, bring axes! I'll lead the way.
             I've changed my mind.
             I did it and I'll undo it.   1290
             Life, I'm afraid, is best spent
             maintaining the established laws,
             for these are moored safe and steady.

             They hurry out to the west, where the sun is now very low.
                    The MESSENGER *leads* KREON *who leads the rest.*

CHORUS   You, god of many names,
             the pride of Theban virgins,
             and son of the deep thunder of Zeus;
             Protector of Italy's glory
             and ruler of Eleusis whose valleys embosom all mankind;
             Dionysos, Bacchus! Your home is Thebes,
             the motherland of your worship,   1300
             beside the supple channel of the Ismenos
             on the soil where the dragon's teeth were planted.

             Above the double cliffs—
             like dazzling flame through vapor,
             through ranks of your nymphs you are perceived—
             and near the Kastalian fountain.

Descending ivied slopes of Euboia, down mountains, rivers
　　　　banked
with the green of numerous clustered vines,
accompanied by the worship
of words and anthems that themselves are immortal,   1310
you are coming to visit Thebes, the city

you honor higher than all others,
here, where lightning was your father.
Now that a violent sickness
holds the nation and all its people,
come, over the slope of Parnassos,
over the groaning channel,
walk here and heal us.

The stars are dancing; they pant fire.
Night is talking. You're their leader.   1320
Boy god and child of Zeus,
master, show us your face; attended
by trains of your nymphs who in madness
dance till the night is ended,
treasurer, Bacchus.

　　　　　　　　　The MESSENGER *returns from the west.*

MESSENGER　Noblemen of Thebes,
　　　　it is impossible ever to praise or to criticize
　　　　any period of a human life.
　　　　Fortune elevates and fortune tumbles
　　　　the fortunate downward and the luckless aloft.   1330
　　　　Once affairs have been determined
　　　　even prophecy cannot assist mortal men.

　　　　Once, in my opinion, Kreon was enviable.
　　　　He had saved our fatherland from its enemies,
　　　　had seized the monarchy,
　　　　and now ruled absolutely,
　　　　flourishing proud in his station and his high-born sons.

But now he has lost everything.
For indeed, when men have forfeited their pleasures,
they are not alive, but the living dead.   1340

To be sure, if you desire it,
gain wealth and power,
live in regal fashion.
However, should the pleasure of such a life be lost,
I, at least, would not purchase the rest,
not if the shadow of smoke were its price.

KORYPHAIOS Under what new burden must our king stand,
and his family? What is it?

MESSENGER The dead,
and the living liable for their dying.

KORYPHAIOS Who is dead? Who is responsible?   1350

MESSENGER Haimon has been destroyed.
Blood shed by one blood.

KORYPHAIOS His father? Himself?

MESSENGER He, himself, in anger at his father.

                        EURYDICE appears in the palace door.

KORYPHAIOS Teiresias was right. All he said has come true.

MESSENGER That is the state of affairs.
It is for you to deliberate upon them.

KORYPHAIOS Wait. Look:
Eurydice, Kreon's wife, leaving the palace.
Perhaps she has heard about her boy . . .   1360
maybe it's only by chance.

EURYDICE Oh, citizens, here you all are.
I was going out to pray;
then I heard you talking.

I was unlocking the door.
I wanted to go to the temple of Pallas
to speak to the goddess.
Then I heard things you were saying.

Something was wrong,
about my own home.   1370
I was frightened.
I tried to lean on something.
My maids were holding me:
I must have fainted.

What were you saying?
Tell it over, to me this time.
Please, go ahead.
I know what grief is.
I can hear more.

MESSENGER My queen, dear lady,   1380
I was present, so I know;
and I shall not omit a word of the truth.
Indeed, why should I soften the story for you,
only to be shown a liar subsequently?
The truth is always the proper thing.

Serving as guide,
I personally attended your royal consort
to the far side of the plain
where the mangled body of Polyneices
still lay, unpitied, where the dogs had dragged it.   1390
We prayed to the goddess of the crossroads and to Pluto
to contain their anger and to bless us;
we bathed and sanctified the body;

then, together with budding twigs we tore down,
burned the remains,
and heaped him a barrow of earth of his homeland,
straight and lofty.
The we proceeded to the maiden's tomb,
a bridal chamber spread with stone.

Even from afar, one of us heard a voice—   1400
shrill weeping, an echo from the tomb—
and he came to our lord Kreon and informed him.
As Kreon approached, the cry hovered about him,
ever nearer, and he moaned then, and shouted:
"Oh, no! Am I a prophet too?
Is this the most luckless road I've ever gone?
'Father'—my son's voice!
Run ahead, men, as fast as you can, up to the tomb!
Some of the stones have been pulled down: get inside!
If that is Haimon's voice I hear . . .   1410
Maybe the gods are robbing me!"

Our master was in despair.
We obeyed him and looked inside.
We saw her down at the tomb's end,
hanged by the neck,
a noose made from her linen robe;
and him, his arms around her waist;
bewept his bride and their lost love,
and his father who had caused this.

Then his father saw him, and cried,   1420
went toward him, cried and called out:
"What did you do? What are you thinking?
What hurt you so? Don't die! Come out!
I'm begging you! On bended knees!"
But the boy looked, wild-eyed, around at him:
spat in his face; not one word;
but drew his sword.

His father dodged and ran back;
so he missed, then turned on himself,
curled over the blade and drove it into his side.   1430
He was still conscious.
His arms flowed about the girl;
he held her and tried to breathe
and breathed out a rush of blood;
and the red drops were on her white cheek.

Now the dead lie in the arms of the dead.
They have been wedded in the house of Death.
Kreon has shown there is no greater evil
than men's failure to consult and to consider.

Exit EURYDICE

KORYPHAIOS   The lady is gone,   1440
returned without a word, good or bad.
What do you think it means?

MESSENGER   I don't know; but I have faith in her.
I believe that she prefers to mourn her son
in her own home.
She is intelligent. She will not do wrong.

KORYPHAIOS   I don't know.
I think that too much silence is more serious
than futile outcries.

MESSENGER   Very well, I shall find out.   1450
Possibly she concealed something,
kept it and contained it in her heart.
I'll follow her. You are right—thank you:
excessive silence, to be sure, is sometimes grave.

MESSENGER *goes into the palace. By now the scene is as dark
as at the beginning of the drama.*

KORYPHAIOS But look, there, he is coming, the king, Kreon.
He carries the token of his own
misdeed, of his own delusion.

KREON enters, from the left, bearing HAIMON's body.

KREON Mindless, hard, deadly crime!
Look: the killer and kill, a father and son.
Poor and worthless counsel, my own.   1460
My boy, young,
and death come soon.
Gone, gone!
I was wrong, not you.

KORYPHAIOS Now you see what Justice is. Too late, it seems.

KREON I have learned, and am ruined.
It was a god. Then, right then!
Hit me, held me, heaped heavy on my head;
shaken on savage paths;
joy trampled;   1470
and for all men, futile struggle.

Enter MESSENGER.

MESSENGER My lord, you have come with grief
like money, in your hands;
and now, in your home, you will see there is more.

KREON What more is left? What's worse?

MESSENGER Your wife, sir, this boy's mother . . .
fresh wounds . . . She is dead.

KREON Ruthless last harbor, death!
Why, when I am destroyed, destroy me again?
Pain and evil! Tell me the worst,   1480
please, young man.

A new victim?
What? What?
Now my wife, so soon?

KORYPHAIOS Now we can see. They're bringing her out.

Slaves lay EURYDICE's *body before the altar in front of the palace.*

KREON I do see: there's no pity.
Where is the end? Where now? Where?
I just held my child, here in my own hands.
Look, there's a second dead.
Grief doubled.   1490
For all sons, all mothers, torture.

MESSENGER On an altar, bent on a sword,
she shuts her eyes in peaceful blackness.
First Megareus, the older son, dead a hero;
and today Haimon:
she wept for both, and at the end
cursed you for both sons' dying.

KREON No, no!
I'm rising on horror, and horror flies.
Why don't you hack me down?   1500
Has someone a sword?
I and grief are blended. I am grief.

MESSENGER You are responsible for her death as well.

KREON How did she die?

MESSENGER When she learned what happened to the boy,
she struck herself, her own hand.

KREON Nobody else; it's my fault.
I killed you. Me, really me.
Men, take me away.

Hurry, take me out of the way.   1510
I'm nobody. I'm nothing.

KORYPHAIOS Hurry? A worthy suggestion, if worth—
or value or profit—exists in evil.
In the midst of evil, done fast is done best.

KREON No more!
The end will be welcome, the final day.
Why don't you come at last?
I'm waiting for doom.
I don't want to see another day.

KORYPHAIOS The future waits, the present claims action.   1520
Your fate is in the care of those who can care for you.

KREON Everything I still want I just now prayed for.

KORYPHAIOS Then pray for nothing more.
No man escapes the grief that awaits him.

KREON Take me away, a poor fool.
I killed you both, son and wife.
No, nowhere to look,
not to lean, but slides from my hands.
It leaps on me, it crushes.

MESSENGER *and servants lead him out slowly, to the right.*

CHORUS (*by pairs, following* KREON) To be sensible and to be pious   1530
are the first and last of happiness. . . .

For their grand schemes or bold words
the proud pay with great wounds. . . .

And great wounds before today
have taught sense even to the aged. . . .

NOTES ON THE TEXT
APPENDIX
GLOSSARY

NOTES ON THE TEXT

In these notes I have referred, by author's name only, to the following studies:

S. N. Adams, *Sophocles the Playwright* (Toronto, 1957)

C. M. Bowra, *Sophoclean Tragedy* (Oxford, 1944)

R. F. Goheen, *The Imagery of Sophocles'* Antigone (Princeton, N.J., 1951)

G .M. Kirkwood, *A Study of Sophoclean Drama* (Ithaca, N.Y., 1958)

H. D. F. Kitto, *Form and Meaning in Drama* (London, 1956)

I. M. Linforth, *Antigone and Creon* (Berkeley and Los Angeles, Calif., 1961)

C. H. Whitman, *Sophocles* (Cambridge, Mass., 1951)

6-8 the ceremony . . . *that began with Oedipus* First suggested here by Antigone, and amplified soon by Ismene (56-72), this theme of a noble house shaken with crime and shattered by the gods prepares the "religious" interpretation of the ensuing action which is offered again by the Chorus (see 729-38; 1003-7; and notes on 576-7 and 1003-7).

It is interesting to conjecture to what degree a contemporary audience would have seen the effects of an hereditary curse in the behavior of Antigone and of Kreon. This would not mean that they saw the persons of tragedy as puppets operated by the gods or as machines tuned by destiny. The concepts of fate and of character may be considered complementary. Both the probable impression of the first hearers, and the characters' thoughts shown at any moment in the play, must be seen as parts of Sophocles' intention, and not as the whole of his understanding.

For the mythological background of 1-20, and of the play as a whole, see Appendix, p. 77 ff.

33 *a tasty meal for vultures*   Antigone's ". . . friends . . . treated as enemies" (14-15) returns to the mind. It was unusual so to mistreat even the enemy dead. The Athenians buried the fallen Persians after Marathon on the grounds that piety required it. A traitor, as Polyneices was, might be denied burial in his homeland, but not burial itself. The people of Athens would certainly have seen Kreon's edict as cruel revenge, illegitimate and patently tyrannical. (See Linforth on Kreon's first speech, pp. 188-93; notes on 227-9, 231, 1389-98, and 1415.)

52-125 *my brother and yours . . . Think of Oedipus . . . senseless . . . bury him, now . . . hate you the more . . . as an enemy*   Antigone seems (52-3) to state a creed: that kinship demands service in death as in life. In 78-81, Ismene agrees with this principle, though she begs off out of fear. In reply (99-101), Antigone reveals her immediate motive, which is love. Antigone's rightness may be called "instinctive" because her love impels her to right thought and action. The "wisdom," on the contrary, and "sense" which urge safety are, in this special tragic situation, inimical to morality and to love. This is why Antigone can answer Ismene's persuasion with threats of hatred (109, 116-18). See notes on 462-3 and 550-73, and cf. note on 33.

Adams typifies Antigone in these words (p. 45): "The tragic history of her family has centred upon all its members, alive and dead, her defensive affection . . . and when this opportunity to do a service to her dead brother is presented to her it is not a question of choosing between the laws of the gods and the laws of man. She has no choice." Whitman (pp. 82-3) finds that Antigone "with her precise and unshakeable perception of divine law, is the embodiment of the heroic individual in a world whose institutions cannot change but have usurped a right to existence apart from the justifiable interest of the citizens. For such an individual every moment of life is tragic. . . ."

On the background of 57-72, see Appendix.

126-95 *Parodos*   The parodos, or entry song of the Chorus, does several things. From a beginning that seems a simple chant of thanksgiving, there emerges a résumé of peril and terror which makes the final, joyous outburst sinister.

The allies Polyneices summoned (140) were more formidable than Polyneices himself. Kapaneus and the other Argive leaders command the action of the ode. When the sons of Oedipus reappear, briefly, it is to share a "twin death" (177-85). The salvation of Thebes is stained with fratricide. Thebes defeats Argos, but destroys herself.

Kapaneus (see Appendix) is at first a man in armor (134); quickly he becomes a bird of prey (141-2). The whole enemy, then, is a ravenous beast (150-1). Ares and Zeus intervene. The monster bird is snared; Thebes, whose noble families claimed descent from Ares' dragon son, is avenged. Kapaneus, blasted to earth, turns out to have been a man merely. The moral (159-76) is a familiar one: pride and its chastisement. But the fall of Kapaneus probably foreshadows the recklessness and ruin of Kreon, whose entry on stage the end of the ode announces. The foreign enemy introduces the enemy at home.

The Chorus' statement that divine aid has saved Thebes is remembered in irony late in the play. One is informed (1170) that Kreon's impiety has sickened the nation. Kreon asserts (1467-9) that his error and ruin were the work of a god. Furthermore, the present invocation of Dionysos (186-95), a call to rejoicing, prepares the way for later song; for when Kreon has gone forth in a vain effort to undo his misdeeds, the Chorus again address Dionysos (1294-1325) but this time prays that he heal the nation's "violent sickness." The prayer is not answered. (See note on 1294-1324.)

205-13 *Out of all the citizens, I have summoned you . . . firm counsel . . . I am king* What Kreon demands now is rather confirmation than advice. Only much later (1271-86) does he seek counsel. Kreon emphasizes that the Chorus is a select group of loyal courtiers, king's men whose support any reigning monarch could rely upon. Kreon is right: until his collapse (1275), the "old men" remain submissive. (See note on 469. Cf. 1455-7; 1465; 1512-14.)

219 *locked in silence and vague fear* Cf. 617, where Antigone applies similar language to the Chorus.

222-3 *And he who cherishes . . . is nothing* Does Kreon intend this to refer to supposed supporters of Polyneices? To the late Polyneices himself? One thinks of Antigone, in anticipation. Later (1511) the words return against Kreon.

227-9; 231 *When she is steady . . . we can love . . . more laws akin to those* The ship of state metaphor is one of many references to the sea and sailing in this play; see 104 and 662; 417-19; 723-8. Compare especially Haimon's argument to Kreon, 866-7, Teiresias', 1143-4, and Kreon's late outburst (1478-9), "Ruthless last harbor, death . . ." See also note on 52-125; Goheen, pp. 48-9; note on 1294-1325.

One must question Kreon's proposition that love follows second to the state, which provides safety. Does not the state rather depend for its cohesion, and consequently its stability, upon the ties of love? See notes on 550-73, 719-62, 1294-1325.

Again: the proclamation concerning the sons of Oedipus is not akin to the two principles Kreon has formulated. Linforth states this strongly (pp. 189-90):

It is not easy to see how Creon considers the case of Polyneices as germane. He has said, in effect, that there are two reasons why Polyneices should not be buried: first, because he must put the interest of the state before the interest of a friend; and second, because the state is threatened with danger which requires prompt action. In both reasons it is assumed that his motive is a sense of public duty. But how will he benefit the state by denying Polyneices burial? . . . In view of the obscurity of the causal relation between the preamble and the decree, the absence of any statement of what Creon hopes to accomplish, and the inadequacy of motive, we are left with only one way to explain his conduct. It seems certain that the spectators would understand him to be actuated by the instinctive feeling . . . that one should do good to his friends and harm to his enemies.

Kreon has treated fellow citizens, friends, and family as enemies (14-15) by denying the claim of kinship, which is a command to sympathy. Polyneices was no less kin to Kreon than was Eteokles. Kreon's confusion regarding love and the state is tangential to his basic error, which is a denial of love. When Haimon says Kreon "could rule a desert right" (890), one thinks that Kreon, by renouncing love, has denied the state as well. It is noteworthy that the Greek philia denotes kinship and friendship together with love, passionate, parental, and proprietary. (See note on 550-73 and Introduction II.)

Bowra, on the other hand, allows (p. 69) that Kreon's refusal of burial to Polyneices is "the logical consequence of a belief that his city demands a man's highest loyalty," but goes on to assert that, on another level, Kreon is wrong (pp. 70-1): "From a Greek point of view Creon errs because he assumes that reasons of state justify him in denying their due to the gods. He neglects the distinction between what is due to them and what is due to men, between what is holy and what is merely just."

247-52; 255 *These opinions . . . us survivors . . . you can put on duty* The Chorus submit to Kreon as king, and instead of commenting on his edict, point to his power. Amazing that the old nobles actually suppose, for a moment, that Kreon wants them to guard Polyneices' corpse, and that they do not flatly refuse, but make an excuse. (See above, note on 205-13.)

262 *A Sentry* Undoubtedly a rustic "type," the Sentry is neither a clown nor a low character. He has been thought the former chiefly because of his hesitancy, and the latter because of his frankness. As for the first, I doubt that anyone will today detect comedy in a poor man's fear of a tyrant. Grim humor is surely present; it consists in the curious contrast of Kreon with the Sentry. The Sentry understands that his message is portentous, while Kreon can only imagine mercenary conspiracies. The Sentry understands both himself and Kreon, but Kreon, who has just misrepresented himself to the Chorus, equally mistakes the Sentry. As to frankness: the clear sight of the Sentry, which he shows in describing the first burial (314-26), comes forth as honest, analytic keenness when he concludes that he is "the kind of man/that puts everything second to his own safety" (536-7). Kreon seldom makes an accurate observation of others, of facts, or of himself (but cf. note on 205-13). The Sentry may well be terrified of the power of a man who cannot tell what is right and what is wrong.

302 *a blockade* Military figures of speech, appropriately, frequent this play, and are especially characteristic of Kreon. Antigone's reference (10) to Kreon's decree has already been mentioned (notes on 33, 227-9) as a clue to the basic difference between her and him. Ismene's plea (74) that she and her sister are "unfit to battle men" once more directed attention to Kreon's nature. What Kreon tells Haimon (809-24) shows his confusion of civil with military norms. His insulting address (1193-5, "Old man, . . . new to me") to Teiresias is so clearly recognized for what it is, that the prophet ends his revelation in similar terms (1260-3, "You have hurt me . . . running"). Kreon understands such language, and begins to see (1283-4) that he "must not fight . . . against fate." (See Goheen, pp. 19-26.)

304-49 *the First Burial* This event remains, as was intended, mysterious. The Sentry's investigative acuity fails him: for want of evidence, he is content to admit that he and his fellows thought a miracle had occurred (314-21). The Chorus think so too (350-1). But when Antigone is cap-

tured, and accused of twice burying Polyneices, she does not deny it
(530-1). It is therefore generally assumed that she had first hastily
sprinkled the body with dust, a token burial, then, unaware of the
discovery and uncovering, returned to complete the ceremony.

On the other hand, the proposition that the Athenian audience,
like the Chorus, would have interpreted the Sentry's account in terms
of divine intervention, has much merit. Recalling the prologue, one
would surely expect that the Sentry has come to report that Antigone
has buried Polyneices. Instead, strange things are told. There is mystery for all but Kreon, whose quick answer reveals only his own de-
fects. Even after line 531, Sophocles' contemporaries could continue
to suppose the first burial was the work of gods; for Antigone no more
confirmed her responsibility for both burials than she denied it for
either.

It should be remembered that dualism and ambiguity are of the
essence both of the mythological background and of the poetic struc-
ture of this play. (See Adams, pp. 47-50; Kitto, pp. 152-7; and Linforth, pp. 194-6, 200-1, 253.)

352-71 *Stop . . . that corpse . . . gods honoring . . . Impossible . . . certain
men . . . I'm positive* Kreon is positive about what he cannot know,
what the gods think about a dead criminal. The assertion that Polyneices intended to burn temples (358-60; cf. 237-8), given as reason
for the gods' unconcern, is both an unwarranted assumption and an
impious presumption to knowledge of the gods' minds. Kreon is again
applying mundane standards to deity; worse, he is justifying acts for
which he alone is responsible, by means of this politicized theology.
(See notes on 227-9, 231, 262, 469, 796-802, 934-41, 1201-5.)

373-91 *Money* Kreon insists his imagined enemies are mercenary. People who
wish to communicate with him—Antigone, Haimon, Teiresias, and at
last the Chorus—must sometimes talk in terms of money. (See 260,
"price"; 402-7; 565-70, "profit"; 1190; 1199-1200; 1235; 1512, "worthy,"
"worth.")

414-55 *First stasimon* The Chorus now see that though the war is over, war cannot be forgotten; that, for men, there is always war: between power
over environment and natural limits, between the need to help and
the need to harm.

Why the elders see this just now is not quite clear. The burial of
Polyneices, if a human being did it, was an ingenious deed and a reck-
less one.

Kreon's accusations, if well founded, would indicate general sedition. Polyneices' treason lost him his home. Kreon has broken a law of the gods by exposing a body. Any one of these facts could prompt the Chorus to reconsider the dangers to which man is born.

As so often, the Chorus say more than they know. In 368 ff., Kreon has spoken of the "conspirators" as though they were domestic animals. In 581-3, he compares Antigone's defiance of his decree to the recalcitrance of a wild horse, which discipline can break; when he orders her punishment he says (936) to "leave her enough fodder only . . ." Now, singing prophecy they do not realize, the old courtiers establish a comparison between the mastery mankind holds over horses and oxen, and the kind of control Kreon is seeking to impose on the Thebans. Kreon risks much; but so has mankind. If Kreon is impious, so has the human species been in daring to plow Earth, "first of the gods." The effort has been wonderful for its successes, but is terrible in two ways: it must end in death, and may first turn to evil (see note on 1099-1134).

The Chorus say that failure to keep the laws of this world bound to divine justice turns the ruler into an exile; this formula will turn out to be applicable to Kreon and to Antigone equally. Kreon disregards justice, and loses his home and throne. Antigone despises unjust law, and is exiled by Kreon from all companionship (see 1000-2, 1015-19, 1039-40). Both suffer for recklessness; but these tragic persons are no more daring than that humanity which risks a way on the winter sea.

462-3 laws of the king . . . senseless   See above, notes on 52-125 and 205-13; also 70-81; and notes on 550-73 and 576-7. The theme of "wisdom," "prudence," "good sense," etc., with their opposites, gains prominence as the play proceeds. (See also notes on 657-91, 692-710, 796-802, 1057-68, 1325 ff., 1361 ff., 1530-end.)

469 just in time   A remark that can be taken as casual; yet Kreon's succession to the throne, a by-product of disaster, doubtless a surprise to himself, was a coincidence. See his words at 205-13: "out of all the citizens . . . I am king." There, he has seemed to be demanding support where he could best expect it; it is probable that he also sought the continuity of order the Chorus represent.

Kreon's self-doubt, which fails to make him prudent, does make him arbitrary and suspicious. Kreon is in fact an ordinary man, too small to wield the kingly power, which corrupts and ruins him. When Antigone told Ismene (43-4) that she would have to "prove you are as brave . . . as you were born to be," she (more literally) asked her either to prove her "nobility" or show herself "a bad offspring from good stock." Ismene failed the test of heroism. When Kreon, of royal lineage, becomes a crude tyrant, he fails a similar test which he has set for himself (214-16).

534-7 **When you go free . . . his own safety** This self-analysis needs to be contrasted with Kreon's lack thereof. Again the Sentry shows that he, who "speaks in the homely and vivid manner of his class" (Linforth), knows himself, and knows how to live for better or worse within his limitations. (See above, notes on 262 and 469.)

550-73 **Zeus . . . Justice lives among . . . made infallible . . . one man and his principles . . . pain I do not feel now** The laws that Kreon spoke of in 214-16 were laws that he would make, based on his "principles," and are also the "pronouncements" which the elders of Thebes so oddly misunderstood (254-5). In the parodos, the Chorus distinguished local and divine law, however (450-5). (See also above, note on 414-55, and below, note on 576-7.) Zeus has ordered that men bury their kin, and Zeus is supreme god of the world of light; Justice—embodied in tradition, resident among the dead, who are the majority of mankind—maintains the same injunction. Celestial and chthonic powers are, here, in accord.

Antigone implies all this. Then she speaks of pain worse than death. "Here," as Linforth says (p. 203), "at last she states precisely the law she has obeyed. It is because Polyneices is her brother that she must not fail in her duty. She has not said . . . that all other Thebans were bound by the same obligation to disobey the godless edict." One notices that Antigone actually gives two separate reasons for her act: first, that Zeus' everlasting laws seemed more worthy of being obeyed than Kreon's, and second, that her loyal feelings were imperative. Her pious decision resulted from her loyalty; her piety merely proved to her that Kreon was unjust. Antigone sees the law of personal responsibility, on which good government must be based, so vividly that she cannot explain it in terms of political platitude (that Kreon would understand) and only partly in terms of religious myth (which the Chorus can appreciate). She can say only that she could not have borne the suffering that disobedience of such law would have brought her. (See notes on 52-125, 1003-24, and 1057-68. In 86-96, we heard a similar argument, in reverse order, which also uses duration as a standard, and pivots on "devotion" equated with personal loyalty.)

576-7 *her father's child . . . his troubles*   Antigone suggests divine motives for her act; the Chorus offer a counter-interpretation, also theological. Antigone, like Oedipus, is obstinate; perhaps, like him, she is blind to the true situation; finally, she too may be involved in the family curse. (See notes on 6-8, 205-13, and 1003-24.)

583 *master nearby*   See 888, "Nations' belong to the men with power," and note on 828-88.

592-4 *let her be . . . their doom*   With a faint echo of the Chorus' prophecy (453 ff.), Kreon blasphemes and condemns himself with all his family. See note on 227-9, 231, lines 798-802, and note on 796-802.

625-43 *Wasn't his enemy your brother? . . . but to love both together*   This clash quickly repeats the contrasts: Kreon's logic, founded on error, succeeds in debate; then, a solid fact stops its progress. Kreon's errors are familiar. He wrongly supposes that enmity justifies denial of burial; he assumes an unknown, that that enmity survives death. The fact Antigone opposes to this is that she naturally loves both her brothers, and that hatred between them, past or present, in no way affects her love for both. (See notes on 52-125, 227-9, 231, 550-73.)

657-91 *I did it . . . served well . . . Kreon   among the dead*   It is to keep Antigone ("If she is with me now") that Ismene, discarding her "good sense," now falsely confesses. If Antigone repels her rather harshly, it is because she sees the futility of this turnabout. Ismene says she cannot bear life without Antigone's love; but Antigone, "in performing the duty which was incumbent on both alike," has "willingly accepted the very extinction of her life" (Linforth). Ismene has forsaken "wisdom" in favor of love too late, just as Kreon will yield to the "established laws" too late. Ismene and Kreon have this, and will have more "in common": both will live on, desolate. Antigone and Haimon will be joined in love among the dead whom they love and to whom they have been faithful.

692-710 *Two girls . . . your own son . . . This marriage business*   Kreon has sensed the absurdity of Ismene's revision without appreciating its significance. What in Ismene is impulse, in Antigone amounts to "a burning moral faith" (Whitman). Ismene returns to "reason," but pleads for love: here is the first mention of Haimon and the betrothal. Kreon's reply is crass and careless. He has no understanding of love whatever. In this, the scene between Kreon and his son is prepared, and, further, Antigone's sorrowful exit.

719-62 Second *stasimon*   As the old courtiers sing, they are inspired. They intend the first pair of strophes to justify their continued support of Kreon, who has just told them (713) they share in the decision to condemn Antigone. By looking upon her death as a divinely wrought completion of the family curse, they try to exonerate their king and themselves. They recall the recklessness of mankind, as they imagine a wintry ocean (see first *stasimon*, and note on 414-55), and end with a vision of madness which appears reasoned.

   This vision expands. Even real logic will shrink beside the immeasurable and incalculable, as human power vanishes in the radiant force of Zeus. One divine law which man may know is that greatness brings ruin; this law explains the "family curse" in moral terms. Without being aware of it, the Chorus have found a key to both Kreon and Antigone: Kreon is being destroyed by greatness of power, Antigone by goodness of character; Kreon is too small, Antigone too great to escape disaster in this stormy world.

   Finally, the old man—evidently still supposing that their real subject is Antigone alone, the "last root, stock of Oedipus" of the first half of the ode—sing only of Kreon, the man who decided bad is good. The Sentry has already seen and (403-4) said that Kreon could make up his mind without being able to tell true from false. Indeed, both Kreon and Antigone have been affected by greatness, and both are being driven to disaster; but Antigone is right, and Kreon wrong. At the end, it is Kreon's "unjust justice" (1085) that Antigone confidently blames, while Kreon declares that "a god" shook him "on savage paths" (1467-9). In the present prophecy, both statements are foreshadowed.

763 you have no other son   The older son, whom Sophocles calls Megareus and Euripides Menoikios, had died not long before. The story told by Euripides (*Phoen.*, 930-1018) is as follows: While the Argives are besieging Thebes, Teiresias reveals that Ares is angry with the royal line of Thebes, because its founder, Kadmos, killed his dragon son. In atonement, one of that family must now die: Eteokles, Kreon, Menoikios, or Haimon. Teiresias suggests the victim be Menoikios. To deceive Kreon, who would save him, Menoikios pretends he will flee. While Kreon collects money for the escape, Menoikios mounts one of the

towers of the city wall and cuts his throat. (See 1492-7, "On an altar . . . both sons' dying," and note on these lines; also Appendix.)

796-802 I *caught her . . . a leader who lies . . . to Zeus for the bonds of blood . . . general disorder*   More illogical and impious words. Kreon seems to say that her rebellion and his fear of appearing inconsistent are equal and valid reasons for him to kill Antigone. He mocks sacred ties with a crude slogan, as though mercy to one's niece were likely to foment revolution. This outrageous center defines the remarks on the family that precede it, and the rationale of autocracy which follows. Cf. above, note on 302.

828-88 After hearing his father's tyrannical speech (777-824) and the Chorus' cautious support of it (825-7), Haimon speaks like an Athenian democrat. All people, he assumes, have innate intelligence which makes their opinions worthwhile. The tyrant, suspicious and fierce, told only what he wants to hear, has no access to honest opinions, and so cannot replenish his mental resources. He rules alone, therefore, in the void of his lonely mind; imagining he owns a nation, he rules a desert. Athenian democracy in Sophocles' day assumed that government, like the state itself, must belong to all citizens, who must all be free.

It is more surprising that the courtiers are impressed (872-4) by Haimon's statement than that they are hushed by Kreon's appeal to age (875).

934-41 the Pronouncement of Sentence   Antigone had heard (39-41, "Whoever . . . citizens") that the penalty for burying Polyneices would be death by stoning. Until now, Kreon has given no notice that he has changed the decree. What has happened? Kreon appears deranged. He has to be reminded (931-3) that Ismene is innocent. The Chorus prompt him. He utters abrupt, intense phrases. Apparently the break with Haimon has moved Kreon. He speaks as though the god (see note on 719-62) that leads him through delusion to disaster were now driving him to the double sacrilege of which Teiresias accuses him (1243-4). (See note on 1240-53.) If Kreon thinks that, by leaving Antigone food, he will avoid the stain of killing his own kin, he is wrong: he thinks of the form, and violates the law in spirit. (See above, note on 352-71 and references.)

942-57 Third *stasimon*   The old men see that the rift between Kreon and his son was immediately caused by Haimon's love for Antigone. They excuse

Haimon by saying Love (*Eros, Desire*) is a god whose power cannot be evaded even by the other gods. But the arguments Haimon used to plead for Antigone were political, not theological or emotional. The Chorus show why, though again without obviously understanding why: it is because this god Love is a Law, chief of those eternal laws Antigone has relied upon. (See notes on 227-9, 231, 550-73, 625-43.) Love must naturally affect the whole nation and the nation's government; for the gods' justice is fundamental to all human relationships. Just as Antigone's love forced her to disobey Kreon's unjust decree, Haimon's obliged him to try to dissuade his father from tyranny.

As they conclude their song, the courtiers are inspired to mention the harsh aspect of the god Love, Love (as Desire) that destroys, again. When Antigone appears, the Koryphaios (Chorus Leader), for the first time (958), expresses sympathy for her and discomfort with Kreon's laws, the "mandates laid down for here." It seems he expected to see Antigone smiling gently, her eyes lowered in modest desire; but, of course, her eyes are lowered in grief (cf. 339 and 539). This bride is mocked by love. She thinks she must now join the dead, not, as Kreon told Haimon (795), to be a "bride in Hades' household," but as a "spinster" among her parents and brothers (1016). Because she has obeyed Love, Antigone now loses life and the share of love that would have filled life. (See 970-1, "No wedding song . . . birthright"; 1026, "They . . . song"; 1041-2, "To my tomb . . . grave"; 1072-5, "And I never . . . desolate"; 1398-9, "Then . . . stone." The accumulation of associated allusions to death and marriage builds to the climax.)

At the play's end, at least, it is clear that Antigone has suffered for no fault. Her doom, and Kreon's, are blamed on the gods—whether Eros, Zeus, or Ares—or not, as men choose. But no final consistency in divine behavior is revealed. The gods are mysterious. The laws Antigone obeys are, finally, her own; for it is she who obeys them.

965-90 Beginning with 965, ending at 1030, Antigone and the Chorus exchange songs. The whole dirge should be recalled in conjunction with 1458-1535, where Kreon sings and the Koryphaios speaks answers.

Antigone is now exhausted. She has no opponent to provoke; she has no one to mourn for her. Her work done, she can only suffer. The elders say all they can: Antigone has won fame, and has chosen her own death.

Niobe turned to stone in grief for her lost children. Antigone is to be immured in a cave, and loses the children she might have borne.

Niobe, however, had boasted of having more children than Leto, and was punished by Apollo and Artemis for impious presumption. This is the difference between Niobe and Antigone, who in fact was about to suffer for reverence. When the Chorus point out that Niobe was the descendant of a god—as if to say "Niobe was more than you"— and at the same time suggest (989, "living and dying, both") that Antigone too was, somehow, irreverent, Antigone declares they are mocking and insulting her. Actually, the old men have again ignored the point.

(On Niobe, see Introduction II and Appendix; Whitman, pp. 93-4 and 96.)

1003-24 **You were harsh . . . mother and father . . . your own destruction** Kreon has returned. The Chorus try to please him by restating (1003-7) the family-curse theme (see note on 576-7). At least this explanation of Antigone's situation cannot cause Kreon to suspect the courtier's loy- alty. (Presumably the curse does not operate on Kreon, who is not a descendant of Laios.) The Chorus then (1020-4) show appreciation of Antigone's initial dilemma: she had to bury Polyneices out of de- votion, and this devotion was, in effect, a form of piety; but secular power cannot, for any motive, be flouted. The Chorus take a short step toward understanding. (See note on 1530-end. On 1017-18, see Appendix.)

1057-68 **But I was right . . . Polyneices, I honored you** This passage has troubled generations of moderns. Bowra (pp. 93-6) believes the function of these lines is to allow Antigone to show her special devotion for Poly- neices, by comparing her love for him, "the strongest tie she had known," with "the husband who is not yet hers, with children who are not yet born." It is a choice of reality over conjecture. Certainly there is support in ancient folklore for the notion that the "degree of consanguinity" should dictate the degree of loyalty. A brother was "closer" than a son. (See Ovid, *Metamorphoses* VIII, 260-525. The concept, very much alive in fifth-century Athens, belongs to the "pre- Homeric" stratum of thought, specifically feminine, which reckons kinship from the womb. This same circle of ideas tends to emphasize the chthonic deities—Mother Earth, Hekate, Dionysos, and the hu- man dead—and to locate Justice, often as Earth or Earth's daughter, in the netherworld. Cf. 550-1; note on 550-73.)

Those who have wished to expunge 1057-68, supposing them an interpolation by Sophocles' son or by some actor, have presupposed the argument to be alien to the character of Antigone, or the style to that of Sophocles. (See Jebb, pp. 164 and 258-63; Whitman, pp. 92-3 and 263-4; note on 942-57.) Conservatives reply in various ways. I can see no reason for removing from any text a passage that has good manuscript authority unless that passage is unquestionably bogus or is meaningless.

One feels, in reading these lines, that Antigone, within the limits of her experience, is right. She had no real choice: now she must reaffirm her faith, however, because imminent death has weakened her (see notes on 942-57, 965-90). The argument seems, at first, mechanical, almost an absurdity in the manner of Kreon. But the emotion that moves the thought is plain enough: imaginings of what might have been, if Kreon had never issued his edict, must be answered with other imaginings, and so exorcized. The marriage Antigone has lost could have ended in widowhood, and the loss of her children. But even such a loss would have been less certain than the death of Polyneices. How, then, could she have failed Polyneices?

Antigone's reasoning does not satisfy, but her sincerity does. She has acted intuitively from the beginning (see notes on 52-125 and 550-73), and has not been able to explain this, in alien terms, to Kreon or to the Chorus. Her present utterance is as directly emotional as any earlier attempt to explain; but it is dressed in terms of "reason." How often, when one is right and others are powerful, does one descend to using the methods of those others? Being right, and so descending, one usually fails. Antigone, if here she stoops to explain, fails no worse in her reasoning this once than Kreon and the Chorus customarily do.

1086-7 *The same . . . this girl* Contrast 958-64. (See notes on 205-13 and 1003-24.)

1099-1134 Fourth *stasimon* Danaë and Lykurgos were both "yoked." One thinks at once of Kreon's strange use of animal imagery, as in 368-70 where he deplores the rebels he thinks have buried Polyneices as men who "shake their heads/instead of properly shouldering the yoke and working with the team,/which is the one way of showing love to me." (See also first *stasimon* and note on 414-55, and 581-3.) Not only is Kreon's idea of harnessing men striking, his connection of it with the notion of love is frightening (see notes on 227-9, 231 and 942-57).

Danaë was "yoked," that is locked, in a tower by her father, Akrisios, king of Argos, who feared a prophecy that he would be killed by his grandson. In her prison Danaë was visited by Zeus in the form of a golden rain. She bore Perseus, who eventually did kill Akrisios. 1099-1106 seems to imply that though Kreon has bound Antigone, her reward will be "golden glory" (see 847), while he will suffer a terrible fate despite his power.

Lykurgos, a Thracian king, had suppressed the rites of the inspired female followers of Dionysos. The god drove him mad. While mad, Lykurgos killed his son; then he was imprisoned by Dionysos. 1110-20 can imply that for abusing Antigone, who was inspired by Love to divine obedience, Kreon may lose his mind, and regain it too late.

Danaë was "yoked," like Antigone, by a human being; Lykurgos, by a god. This, Kreon will learn (see 1467-71; note on 719-62) when he discovers "what Justice is" (1465), "too late," as the Chorus will say. A nameless god yokes Kreon to work for his own ruin. But now the old courtiers do not know this. When shown clearly by Teiresias (1170; 1217; and 1240-53) the madness of Kreon, the sickness of the nation, the Chorus will turn to Dionysos for healing (see 1294-1325, and note on these lines; cf. note on 126-95).

War is not forgotten. Like Love, Ares, the god of war, does not always bring joy with victory (cf. notes on 126-95, 414-55, and 942-57).

The tale contained in 1121-34 is not clear. Phineus, another Thracian king, married Kleopatra, a daughter of the North Wind, Boreas. She bore him two sons. He divorced and imprisoned her and permitted his new wife, Eidothea, to blind the two sons and shut them up in a tomb. The blinding is witnessed by Ares. The blinded eyes of the boys are "unforgiving," their wounds "damning." We are told elsewhere that Phineus was later blinded by the gods. The Chorus have returned to the theme of the House Cursed by Heaven, and to a world of violence that has so recently been their world.

Antigone, imprisoned, can now think of the two sons of blind Oedipus, her dead brothers—as Kleopatra could remember her husband and sons—and know how harsh Fate is. But Kleopatra could not help her sons, and would not pity their father. Her own father, who had tended her in caves that were his palaces, is not comparable to Oedipus, a god to a man. Can we suppose the caves of Boreas correspond to the palace of Thebes? Kleopatra's mother came to Boreas' palace from Athens, and Antigone returned to Thebes from Athens after Oedipus' death.

Again: we are about to see Eurydice's death, a result of the deaths of Megareus and Haimon (see note on 763). Ares had a part in the death of the former, Kreon in that of both sons. This tempts one to see Kreon in Phineus (as in Akrisios and Lykurgos), Eurydice in Kleopatra.

Many readers have left this ode unsatisfied, often convinced the old gentlemen of the Chorus are confusedly expressing their sorrow, or generally deploring cruelty. (See Goheen, pp. 64-72.)

1140 ff. **Teiresias** No doubt, Teiresias is the representative of the gods, as Haimon is the voice of the people. But both have personality, and speak the truth for personal reasons. Though each is, in his way, inspired, neither prophesies in an ecstasy, as the Chorus do, but rather in full consciousness. While we may find in Haimon, the "democrat," an amateur seer, moved this once, by Love, to speak (see notes on 828-88 and 934-41), Teiresias has an ancient vocation to know and speak the truth. Both begin gentle, end angered. The similarities of their language seem to justify Haimon's stand, and make Teiresias' revelation resonant.

Sophocles may be hinting that the voice of intelligent men is as reliable as an oracle, and that what good people say early, the gods confirm too late; the first ought to be heard to good effect, the latter will be heard as irony. Again: Eros may be as good an oracular deity as Apollo. Certainly the *Antigone* shows no attempt to rationalize the gods' ways, to ignore their existence, to resolve the problem of evil, or to relieve men even of crushing responsibility.

1201-5 *But bury . . . to pollute gods* Final blasphemy and more "reason." Kreon "knows" no human being can pollute gods, but disregards the meaning of the phrase: Men pollute themselves, and are rejected by the gods. (See notes on 352-71, 592-4, 796-802, 934-41.)

1240-53; 1276-7 *Few courses . . . the midst of your crimes . . . release the girl . . . and build a tomb* The time for warning has passed. Here Kreon is forced to know he has been wrong and will suffer. Teiresias speaks of certainties. Neither men nor gods can change what has been done or what will happen. Furies have been generated by crime, and cannot be prevented from destroying the criminal; they are forces which are dissipated only by performing their function, vengeance.

The double crime is a turnabout of nature: exposing the dead, burying the living. Though the first of these justifies Antigone's act, Teiresias' account does not explicitly exonerate Antigone. The seer says nothing of her except that Kreon, by burying her alive, has multiplied tangible evil. The spokesman of the gods is not so much interested in human virtue as in the mechanics of ritual and the physics of piety.

1294-1325 Fifth *stasimon* The state of Thebes, we know, is sick. The old men pray again to the ever-youthful god Dionysos, on behalf of the nation of the dragon's teeth (see notes on 126-95 and 763). Like Ares (1123), Bacchus shall have an aerial view, as he comes, of fine scenery and disaster. He has been invoked in postwar joy; now he is invited to heal the city where Zeus begot him, his city: the appeal is founded on filial loyalty. If the men of the Chorus see little family solidarity in Thebes —the outstanding instance of it has been punished cruelly—they may seek some in heaven.

The contrast between men and gods is reinforced with pictures of sea-crossings. In the first *stasimon*, 416-18, that wonder man was seen daring the wintry ocean; in the second *stasimon*, 720-8, the theme of the "house quaked by the gods" was represented through imagery of a sea storm. When Love was sung, in the third *stasimon*, he was easily "grazing" the deep (945). Now Dionysos walks over the "groaning channel" (1317) from Euboia to Thebes. Just as the virtues men lack can be taken for granted among gods, tasks men undertake to their peril are easy for and natural to deity.

There is also mystery, or at least paradox here. The joyous wine god to whom Thebes turned after Ares left is summoned to the site of his birth by Ares' people. One remembers that the lightning flash of Zeus not only created Bacchus, but destroyed the mother, Semele. This sounds like a parable of sky and earth, alluding too to the struggle of celestial with chthonic deities. One is oddly reminded of the victory torch of Kapaneus and of the bolt that cast him down (159-70). The stars that dance breathe fire.

Finally, the tales of Danaë and of Lykurgos are brought to mind. Dionysos is the "pride of Theban Virgins," worshiped in immortal anthems, attended by trains of maddened nymphs (1295; 1305; 1323-4). The Chorus already have sung of Dionysos' punishment of Lykurgos, who had stopped the orgies of his followers (see 1110-20 and note on 1099-1134). The present song again suggests a comparison between Antigone and the Thracian Bacchantes, and seems to offer hope that the god will vindicate her as he did them. It is a feeble hope. As for Danaë: she "received and stored" Zeus' golden seed (1105), and now Bacchus is addressed as "treasurer." (The Greek wording is even closer.) The Chorus may be praying that in some way the god will not only save, but disburse glory to Antigone. When the Chorus ask Dionysos to "heal" the sick city, one thinks of Kreon, (1170; 1217; 1243-9) and perhaps wonders at the request: Dionysos was not traditionally concerned with healing. The wish seems to be that Kreon will be merely quarantined, like Lykurgos, even that he too may put aside his madness and be well. The Chorus is nourishing, with such pious confidence, the vain longing an audience must feel; but the effect is irony (see note on 1240-53, 1276-7; Linforth, p. 238).

1326 The Messenger   Like the Sentry (see notes on 262 and 534-7) this man is an individual; he too may be compared to and contrasted with Kreon. All three are sententious in speech. The Sentry's country wisdom, which Kreon mocks, is seen to be more effective than the king's autocratic precepts. While Kreon uses cliché to hide his thoughts, the Sentry uses it to discover his. The Messenger employs pompous language and lofty precept to maintain self-control; in this, he resembles both the Sentry and Kreon. His mannerisms are his own: to this translator, the Messenger seems to be young, to lean on what he has learned in school. He is forced, by what he has to tell, to display emotion, however manfully he tries to master it.

The dramatic purpose of these distinctive minor characters, Sentry and Messenger, is, at least in part, to show us ordinary men, to show in turn that Kreon is ordinary, that his heroic heritage fails him or he it. (See note on 469.)

1362 ff. Eurydice   She speaks to fall silent. The queen does not fear emotion, or the truth. Antigone would become queen. . . . An audience would remember Haimon and his father while sharing the stillness of Eurydice, who, like the Messenger, stands between those two and us.

When awful words stopped her, Eurydice intended to visit Pallas Athena. This goddess has a complex nature. Born from Zeus' forehead, she was known by the ancients as a deity of wisdom: right, and so righteous, Pallas Athena was patroness of handicrafts; for skill seemed inseparable from intellect, practical excellence from goodness. Though her wisdom was womanly, and feminine crafts especially her own, Athena was pictured dressed in armor, with shield and spear. Her person was martial. Sometimes men associated her with Ares. Unwedded, she was called "Mother."

If the people of the Antigone must seek wisdom out of war, Queen Eurydice alone has thought of consulting the deity that could best help in the search. Haimon's death, however, has intervened. Only

Haimon and Antigone, the new generation, have appeared to possess the generous rectitude the nation needs. What of Antigone? The princess, remembered at this moment, resembles less the nymphs of Bacchus (notes on 1099-1134 and 1294-1325; see also note on 52-125) than Pallas herself, a virgin goddess whose virtues are peculiarly those of a mother, one who could know and care (cf. 516-18, the Sentry's simile).

1389-98 *body of Polyneices . . . Then we proceeded* Why in this order? We wonder whether Antigone can wait, and find our fear turned to anger. The Chorus said (1276-7) to release the girl and to build Polyneices a tomb; this had been the order of crimes in Teiresias' indictment (1243-7), albeit with emphasis on Polyneices.

The reversal is characteristic of Kreon. What concerns him most is Teiresias' warning that enemy nations, their altars polluted with Polyneices' flesh, would rise against Thebes (1257-9). A human life is less important to Kreon. He refuses to cherish "an individual beyond his homeland" (see 222-3); yet he is nothing (note on 222-3). It is possible that Sophocles' contemporaries would have seen this act as the final shove the gods applied to Kreon to drive him to destruction, to prod his fault to full growth; that is Kreon's opinion (note on 719-62). But it has been "greatness" too, that drove Kreon to disaster (see note on 6-8). The king has still not learned anything.

The form of Polyneices' funeral is curious. The Messenger tells us (1393-7) that the company burned then buried the remains. Earth burial—such as Antigone attempted—implies a return of the dead to Earth, the source of life; some of the fundamental assumptions of the play, most frequently expressed by Antigone, are those of an inhumating people which finds value in the realm of chthonic deities: Dionysos, Persephone, Pluto, Earth, and Justice. (See above, note on 1057-68, and Appendix. The dragon "son of Ares," from which the noble Thebans traced their origin, is clearly a spirit of earth, in the common serpent form also noted in the stories of Kadmos and of Teiresias.) Cremation, by contrast, supposes that the dead lose their earthly characteristics, and tends to favor faith in celestial deities—Apollo, Ares, Athena, Eros, Zeus.

We have heard that by denying Polyneices to the nether gods Kreon has offended the celestials (1172-7; 1202-5). Now Kreon, fatuously doubling the doubled scheme, tries to appease both groups of gods at once.

1415 *hanged* Cf. 62-5, "and Mother . . . twisted life away." When Oedipus' identity became known to her, Jocasta died in this way. (See Appendix.) The hanged dead, deprived of contact with the earth, suffer especially; they are vitiated by loss of the vital contact, and kept in exile from the netherworld.

1436-7 *Now the dead . . . wedded . . . the house of Death* See note on 942-57 and lines noted.

1492-7; 1509-10 *On an altar . . . for both sons' dying . . . Men, take me away. Hurry* See 763 and note on that line. Kreon has made the Sentry (392-3), Antigone and Ismene (714-15), Haimon (922-6), and again Antigone (1034-6) depart from his presence. In the case of each, he drove off something he needed or which was part of himself; now he dismisses what is left. See above, 222-3 and note on those lines.

1530 to end To be sensible (when one can also be pious) and pious (when circumstances favor it) would indeed secure happiness. To Antigone, the second forbade the first. Kreon could, had he had true sense, have been pious; but pride destroyed his reason.

In the final words, "even to the aged," the old courtiers speak for themselves. They misjudged Kreon and Antigone, and not even their own songs, sung inspired, could teach them true, rather than safe sense. One doubts that they have learned even now. Whitman (p. 92) suspects the Chorus is "an intentional symbol of the inadequacy of everyday morality to judge the ultimate questions." (See 1465, which is similarly applicable to both Kreon and Chorus, and, in résumé, notes on 52-125, 205-13, 219, 414-55, 462-3, 576-7, 719-62, 942-57, 965-90, 1003-24, 1086-7, 1099-1134, and 1294-1325.)

APPENDIX

MYTHOLOGICAL CONTEXT OF THE ANTIGONE

Zeus, father of gods and men, assumed the form of a white bull, and by gentle gesture so captivated Europa, daughter of the king of Tyre, that she mounted him. Immediately, he transported her to Crete. The king sent his sons to find Europa; they were not to return without her. One son, Kadmos, after wandering far north, to Thrace, in vain, went to Delphi for divine guidance. Apollo ordered him to abandon the search. Kadmos was destined to found a nation. He was to follow a certain cow: where she lay down, there he should build.

Kadmos obeyed. His "Kadmeia" was the nucleus of the city Thebes, while the surrounding country was called Boeotia, "Cow-land." Kadmos sacrificed the cow to Athena. He required water for purification before the sacrifice could be accomplished, and so sent men to the one spring nearby. The dragon which guarded this spring killed Kadmos' men. Kadmos killed the dragon, which happened to be a son of Ares.

Athena then ordered Kadmos to pull the dragon's teeth and plant them. He did so. Many brothers grew from the land, full-armed. Kadmos threw stones at them. Each blamed the others for the stoning; soon, they leveled spears at one another; at last, only five remained. These founded the noble houses of Thebes.

Kadmos married another child of Ares, Harmonia, whose mother was Aphrodite. One of their daughters, Semele, visited by Zeus in the form of lightning, left a divine son, Dionysos. King Kadmos retired. His successor was his grandson Labdakos.

When Labdakos died, leaving an infant heir, Laios, a nobleman named Lykos became regent. But in time, Lykos made himself king. His neice, Antiope, was seduced by Zeus and gave birth to Amphion

95

and Zethos; for this disgrace, Lykos imprisoned Antiope. Eventually, the sons rescued their mother, and killed Lykos and his wife Dirke (from whose blood sprang the river Dirke, to the west of the city). Amphion and Zethos drove the young pretender Laios from the land.

Besides these royal personages, the first notable grandson of the warriors who were the harvest of the dragon's teeth was Teiresias. In his youth, a magic accident transformed him into a woman; after some years, Teiresias reversed the magic, and thereafter remained a man. It was he, reasonably, whom Zeus and Hera required to judge between them; for each maintained that the opposite sex has more pleasure. When Teiresias said women have nine times the delight of men, Hera blinded him, and Zeus gave him long life and the power of prophecy. Teiresias lived through seven generations of Thebans.

In the fourth generation, then, the land was ruled by Amphion and Zethos. Amphion, a bard, built the walls of the city: stones danced into place to the tune of his harp. He married Niobe, daughter of the Argive king Tantalos. Niobe bore twelve children, and boasted that she was better than the goddess Leto, who had but two; those two, Apollo and Artemis, killed the twelve. Niobe wept until she turned to stone; the stone still weeps there. Amphion took his own life. Zethos, the warlike brother, married Thebe, a nymph of the place, in whose honor he renamed the city. Only the citadel continued to be called Kadmeia.

In the meantime, Laios had grown to manhood. He lived in exile in Argos, enjoying the hospitality of King Pelops, son of Tantalos. He violated this hospitality by abducting Pelops' pretty son. But now, when Zethos died, Laios became king of Thebes. The curse of Pelops, however, pursued him: when Laios had already married Jocasta, he was warned by Apollo that a son by her would one day kill him.

A son was born. Laios had the baby cast out in the mountains. A shepherd found him there, and brought him to Corinth, where the childless king and queen raised him as their own. They named him Oedipus. When he grew up, Oedipus heard he was not his parents' child. He went to Delphi. Apollo told him he was destined to kill his father and marry his mother. Oedipus decided never to return to Corinth. He wandered to Boeotia. There he quarreled, fought with, and killed Laios.

In Thebes, Oedipus found confusion and terror. First, the king had been murdered. Now too, the city was threatened by a monster, the Sphinx. Kreon, the regent, offered the throne and the hand of his widowed sister, Queen Jocasta, to any man who could restore safety to the kingdom. Oedipus destroyed the Sphinx.

After Jocasta had borne Oedipus two sons, Eteokles and Polyneices, and two daughters, Antigone and Ismene, the truth was revealed by Teiresias. Jocasta hanged herself. Expelled by Kreon, his uncle and brother-in-law, Oedipus went to Kolonos, a town in Attica, where he was cared for by Antigone until his death. The sons of Oedipus now agreed to rule in alternate years; while one was king, the other should leave Thebes. The second regency of Kreon ended when Eteokles became king.

In Argos, Polyneices married the daughter of King Adrastos. Eteokles had now decided not to descend from the throne at the year's end after all. Adrastos mustered an army to restore his son-in-law to Thebes. He, Polyneices, Amphiaraos, Kapaneus, and three others were to lead the expedition. Amphiaraos, who foresaw that of their number only Adrastos was destined to survive, was nevertheless persuaded to participate; before the Argive army marched, he instructed his son Alkmaion to destroy Thebes when the right time came.

In Thebes, meanwhile, Teiresias had foretold an Argive victory: Ares, dispenser of the events of war, still held the Kadmeian nation liable for his dragon son's death. Only the sacrifice of a descendant of those first five fratricidal warriors could atone. Megareus (or Menoikios), son of Kreon, climbed the city wall, cut his throat, and fell directly into the dragon's den. This act postponed Thebes' doom.

The men of Argos attacked. Kapaneus stormed the wall Amphion had built with music, and reaching the heights stood with torch in hand and declared that now not even Zeus could keep him out of the city. Zeus struck him with a thunderbolt. This was the signal for Theban victory. Four more Argive commanders fell. Adrastos fled. Eteokles and Polyneices killed eath other.

Now Kreon was king. His first act was to bury the Theban dead; but those of the enemy who had fallen, including Polyneices, he left on the field. Antigone, however, managed to bury her outlawed brother.

What then passed between Antigone and her uncle Kreon is not clear. One version of the tale leaves Thebes peacefully divided on the burial question: partisan sentiment in favor of Eteokles is balanced by sorrow over the fate of Polyneices and by sympathy with Antigone and Ismene. The story Sophocles tells seems to be an original conception. The standard Athenian version of the sequel appears to be this: Adrastos persuaded Theseus, king of Attica, to set matters right.

Defeating Kreon's army, Theseus honorably interred the Argive war dead. Subsequently, Kreon was deposed.

It was the next generation, the eighth after Kadmos, that saw Thebes fall. A new army came out of Argos. Alkmaion, son of Amphiaraos, killed the last Theban king. Since defeat was certain, Teiresias came forward with a plan: to busy the Argives with negotiations and meanwhile, during the night, secretly to evacuate the city. The plan succeeded. Most of the citizens escaped into the countryside. Teiresias himself died on the way.

GLOSSARY

The Appendix, p. 95 ff., gives a fuller account of many persons listed here.

ACHERON, river of Pain, in the kingdom of Hades.
ANTIGONE, daughter of Oedipus and Jocasta.
ARES, god of war; son of Zeus and Hera, father, with Aphrodite, of Harmonia.
ARGOS, a powerful Peloponnesian city-state.
ATHENA (Athene), or Pallas Athena, daughter of Zeus; goddess of wisdom.

BACCHUS, see Dionysos.
BOREAS, the North Wind.
BOSPORUS, strait leading from the Propontis (Sea of Marmara) into the Pontus (Black Sea) past Byzantium.

CROSSROADS, goddess of, see Hekate.

DANAË, daughter of Akrisios, king of Argos; mother, by Zeus, of Perseus.
DEATH, see Hades.
DESIRE, see Eros.
DIKE, or Justice; a minor earth goddess.
DIRKE, or "west river"; a Theban spring.
DIONYSOS, the god Bacchus, manifest in vines, rivers, the veins; son of Zeus by Semele, the daughter of Kadmos and Harmonia.

EARTH, or Mother Earth, "Ge."
ELEUSIS, site of chthonic mystery cult of the Athenians.
EROS, god of love; son of Aphrodite.
ETEOKLES, son of Oedipus and Jocasta.

EUBOIA, large island east of Boeotia.

EURYDICE, wife of Kreon.

FURIES, the Erinyes or Eumenides, avenging spirits, particularly concerned with violations of blood ties.

HADES, "the Unseen," Zeus' brother; king of the netherworld, the "House of Hades." Also known as Pluto "the Rich," as deity of the riches of the earth and hidden treasure.

HAIMON, younger son of Kreon and Eurydice.

HEKATE, a chthonic deity, goddess of the crossroads, where unsanctified dead were buried.

ISMENE, daughter of Oedipus and Jocasta.

ISMENOS, the river east of Thebes.

JOCASTA (Iokaste), sister of Kreon, wife of Laios, mother and wife of Oedipus.

JUSTICE, see Dike.

KASTALIAN FOUNTAIN, on Mount Parnassos; its stream descends through Delphi.

KREON, king of Thebes, brother-in-law of Laios.

LAIOS, king of Thebes.

LOVE, see Eros.

LYKURGOS, Thracian king who persecuted Dionysos' followers.

MEGAREUS, or Menoikios, elder son of Kreon and Eurydice.

MUSES, "the Reminders," daughters of Zeus and Memory; worshiped on Mount Helicon in Boeotia, these goddesses inspired prophecy and the arts.

NIKE, goddess of victory.

NIOBE, daughter of Tantalos, a son of Zeus, king of Argos; wife of Amphion, king of Thebes.

NORTH WIND, Boreas.

OEDIPUS, king of Thebes, son of Laios and Jocasta.

OLYMPOS, a mountain that led to the abode of the celestial deities; thus, the sky.

PAIN, river of, see Acheron.

PALLAS, see Athena.

PARNASSOS, a mountain above Delphi, dwelling of Apollo and the Muses; nearby, Oedipus killed Laios.

PERSEPHONE, an earth goddess, wife of Hades.

PHINEUS, Thracian king, whose two sons were blinded by their stepmother, an act damned by the gods.

PLUTO, see Hades.

POLYNEICES (Polyneikes), son of Oedipus and Jocasta.

SARDIS, ancient capital of Lydia in Asia Minor, where "electrum," white gold alloyed with silver, originated.

TEIRESIAS, Theban prophet.

THEBES, chief city of Boeotia.

THRACE, the south-east part of the Balkan peninsula, home of Ares.

VICTORY, see Nike.

WAR, see Ares.

WEST RIVER, see Dirke.

ZEUS, chief god, lord of oaths and loyalty, a celestial.